udents as raprofessional Staff

Steven C. Ender, Roger B. Winston, Jr., *Editors*

NEW DIRECTIONS FOR STUDENT SERVICES

URSULA DELWORTH and GARY R. HANSON, *Editors-in-Chief*

Number 27, September 1984

Paperback sourcebooks in
The Jossey-Bass Higher Education Series

Jossey-Bass Inc., Publishers
San Francisco • Washington • London

Steven C. Ender, Roger B. Winston, Jr. (Eds.).
Students as Paraprofessional Staff.
New Directions for Student Services, no. 27.
San Francisco: Jossey-Bass, 1984.

New Directions for Student Services Series
Ursula Delworth and Gary R. Hanson, *Editors-in-Chief*

New Directions for Student Services (publication number USPS
449-070) is published quarterly by Jossey-Bass Inc., Publishers.
Second-class postage rates paid at San Francisco, California,
and at additional mailing offices.

Correspondence:
Subscriptions, single-issue orders, change of address notices, undelivered
copies, and other correspondence should be sent to Subscriptions,
Jossey-Bass Inc., Publishers, 433 California Street, San Francisco
California 94104.

Editorial correspondence should be sent to the Editors-in-Chief,
Ursula Delworth, University Counseling Service, Iowa
Memorial Union, University of Iowa, Iowa City, Iowa 52242
or Gary R. Hanson, Office of the Dean of Students,
Student Services Building, Room 101, University of Texas
at Austin, Austin, Texas 78712.

Library of Congress Catalogue Card Number LC 83-82741

International Standard Serial Number ISSN 0164-7970

International Standard Book Number ISBN 87589-788-6

Cover art by Willi Baum

Manufactured in the United States of America

Ordering Information

The paperback sourcebooks listed below are published quarterly and can be ordered either by subscription or single-copy.

Subscriptions cost $35.00 per year for institutions, agencies, and libraries. Individuals can subscribe at the special rate of $25.00 per year *if payment is by personal check.* (Note that the full rate of $35.00 applies if payment is by institutional check, even if the subscription is designated for an individual.) Standing orders are accepted. Subscriptions normally begin with the first of the four sourcebooks in the current publication year of the series. When ordering, please indicate if you prefer your subscription to begin with the first issue of the *coming* year.

Single copies are available at $8.95 when payment accompanies order, and *all single-copy orders under $25.00 must include payment.* (California, New Jersey, New York, and Washington, D.C., residents please include appropriate sales tax.) For billed orders, cost per copy is $8.95 plus postage and handling. (Prices subject to change without notice.)

Bulk orders (ten or more copies) of any individual sourcebook are available at the following discounted prices: 10–49 copies, $8.05 each; 50–100 copies, $7.15 each; over 100 copies, *inquire.* Sales tax and postage and handling charges apply as for single copy orders.

To ensure correct and prompt delivery, all orders must give either the *name of an individual* or an *official purchase order number.* Please submit your order as follows:

Subscriptions: specify series and year subscription is to begin.
Single Copies: specify sourcebook code (such as, SS8) and first two words of title.

Mail orders for United States and Possessions, Latin America, Canada, Japan, Australia, and New Zealand to:
    Jossey-Bass Inc., Publishers
    433 California Street
    San Francisco, California 94104

Mail orders for all other parts of the world to:
    Jossey-Bass Limited
    28 Banner Street
    London EC1Y 8QE

New Directions for Student Services Series
Ursula Delworth and Gary R. Hanson, *Editors-in-Chief*

Contents

Student affairs professionals can take pride in the state of the art of student paraprofessional programs. However, much work remains to be done if quality programs are to be achieved.

Editors' Notes

Student paraprofessional staffing across student affairs departments and agencies has increased steadily during the past ten years. Presently, about three quarters of all student affairs divisions have one or more student paraprofessional programs. Quality programs have six characteristics: They have written program goals; they address the normal developmental needs of college student clients and paraprofessionals; they use written job descriptions to guide the working student paraprofessional; they view recruitment, selection and training as a continuous, integrated process; they practice systematic supervision; and they carry out sound evaluation of staff and programs. Quality student paraprofessional programs affect student clients, the institution, and student paraprofessionals in positive ways.

The purpose of this sourcebook is to survey the extent of paraprofessional programming in student affairs and to provide guidance for the use of paraprofessionals. In Chapter One Steven C. Ender explores factors accounting for the increase in use of paraprofessionals and calls attention to important issues that require attention in paraprofessional programs. Characteristics of quality programming are described, and research documenting the extent to which these program variables have been implemented is discussed. Thus Chapter One presents the basic issues raised by quality paraprofessional programs regardless of setting.

Chapters Two, Three, Four, Five, and Six investigate the use of student paraprofessionals in five program settings. Each chapter addresses the issues—goals, position descriptions, recruitment, selection, training, supervision, and evaluation—in designing and implementing paraprofessional programs and describes innovative programs staffed by student paraprofessionals.

In Chapter Two, Georgine Materniak describes paraprofessional programs in learning centers. She pays special attention to paraprofessional roles in the center, to responsible behavior for learning center paraprofessionals, to administrative and managerial concerns, and to training, supervision, and evaluation.

In Chapter Three, Wesley R. Habley focuses on the role of the student paraprofessional in academic advising. Research findings on paraprofessional effectiveness and client satisfaction are discussed. Advantages of paraprofessional advisors are highlighted, and practices that must be considered when a student paraprofessional advising program is implemented are reviewed.

In Chapter Four, Roger B. Winston, Jr., Marcy S. Ullom, and Charles J. Werring consider the use of paraprofessionals in residence halls. They focus on the philosophy of residential developmental education, on the roles and responsibilities of resident hall paraprofessionals, and on the legal and ethical issues that must be considered when such programs are implemented.

In Chapter Five, Kenneth L. Ender and Gerry Strumpf provide guidance to professionals who must implement orientation programs staffed by student paraprofessionals. A contemporary perspective concerning student orientation is presented. Several types of orientation models are described, and the responsibilities of paraprofessionals within each model are discussed. Issues raised by implementing a student-staffed orientation program are highlighted.

In Chapter Six, Ursula Delworth and Mary Johnson focus on the role of student paraprofessionals in counseling and career centers. They discuss training, supervision, and ethical issues related to use of student paraprofessionals in counseling and career work.

Steven C. Ender concludes the sourcebook with Chapter Seven, in which he addresses issues in the student paraprofessional area that need refinement.

The editors of this sourcebook and the authors of its chapters are indebted to the paraprofessional coordinators who provided descriptions of their programs. Readers are encouraged to contact these individuals for additional information concerning these innovative practices. The coordinators' names and addresses are listed in Appendix A. Appendix B proposes some standards for the use of student paraprofessionals.

A word of appreciation is extended to Pat Brown for her work on the data analysis presented in Chapter One, and Brenda Rieschick and Phyllis Goeckel are to be commended for their endurance and patience in typing chapter drafts.

Steven C. Ender
Roger B. Winston, Jr.
Editors

Steven C. Ender is assistant professor and counselor in the Center for Student Development at Kansas State University. Actively involved in paraprofessional programs throughout his professional career, he has coauthored a training manual for paraprofessionals, and he has also been actively involved in training professionals who desire to implement paraprofessional programs.

Roger B. Winston, Jr., is associate professor in the Department of Counseling and Human Development Services, College of Education, University of Georgia. He has directed a residence hall program, and he currently teaches in the resident assistant training program as part of his teaching responsibilities.

Paraprofessional programs staffed by undergraduate students
help to promote preventive student development practices within
higher education. When properly implemented, paraprofessional
programs have benefits for student clients, the college, and
paraprofessionals.

Student Paraprofessionals Within Student Affairs: The State of the Art

Steven C. Ender

The utilization of undergraduate students as peer helpers within institutions of higher education can be traced to the early history of American colleges and universities. As Materniak points out in Chapter Two, student tutors have been assisting their peers since the colonial period. Powell and others (1969) cite the use of students in residence halls as resident assistants, proctors, hall counselors, and advisors since the turn of the century. Although these early efforts were primarily informal and unsystematic, they established a precedent quite early that students have the potential to be a strong influence on the growth and development of their peers.

This chapter has several purposes. Primarily, it examines the emerging maturity of the student paraprofessional movement within divisions of student affairs. The intention is to provide a state-of-the-art view of undergraduates assisting their peers in the context of preventive, developmental programming. Within this context, several themes are introduced supporting the concept that student paraprofessionals must be regarded as important staff members. Research finds that between 72 percent (Ender and Winston, 1984) and 78 percent (Salovey, 1983) of all student affairs divisions in higher education provide student-staffed programs. Program settings now offering interventions through paraprofessional staffing are described in this chapter, and the rationales for their use are outlined. The research literature

S. Ender, R. Winston (Eds.). *Using Students as Paraprofessional Staff.* New
Directions for Student Services, nò. 27. San Francisco: Jossey-Bass, September 1984.

detailing the effectiveness of paraprofessionals is discussed, and rationales for the success of student-staffed paraprofessional programs are examined.

To support the argument that student-staffed paraprofessional programs are maturing, several themes are explored. A working definition of the student paraprofessional is introduced, and the primary services that a paraprofessional can perform are discussed. Standards for paraprofessional programming are proposed, and a model for implementing student paraprofessional staffed programs is presented. Particular attention is focused on the issues involved in implementing a paraprofessional program—recruitment, selection, training, compensation, supervision, and evaluation—and the ways in which programs implement these program components are detailed. The chapter concludes with a discussion of the legal and ethical issues raised by the use of student paraprofessionals and with some general comments about the future of this programming technique.

Studies Concerning the Utilization of Student Paraprofessionals

As student paraprofessional programming continued to grow, several studies focusing on the extensiveness of this staffing technique were conducted. The first was by Powell (1959), who reported that 67 percent of the survey respondents used upperclassmen in counseling-type roles. The majority of survey respondents reported using student counselors for new student orientation and residence hall work. Student counselors worked primarily in the area of personal and social concerns, assisting students in their general adjustment to the college campus. The reason cited most often by survey respondents for using students as counselors was that they were able to communicate with and be accepted by their peers. Respondents noted also that the work activity was a good learning and leadership opportunity for the student counselors. It is worthy of note that the administrators of these early formalized student paraprofessional programs were skeptical of utilizing paraprofessionals in areas of academic, vocational, religious, and health concerns. Students are now working rather extensively in many of these areas.

Brown and Zunker (1966) conducted the next extensive investigation of student paraprofessionals in higher education during the 1963–64 academic year. These authors found that 65.6 percent of institutions in higher education were utilizing student paraprofessionals. Brown (1977, p. 17) compared the results of Powell's (1959) study with those of Brown and Zunker (1966) and noted: "Comparison of the two studies . . . suggests a developing trend toward using student counselors to provide systematic counseling in the areas of academic adjustment problems and to employ them on a continuing basis in settings other than residence halls." While the majority of paraprofessional utilization continued to be in residence halls and orientation programs, increased utilization was noted in the areas of personal and social counseling, study habits counseling, and subject matter tutoring; religious counseling; educational planning; vocational guidance; and even in psychological test interpretation (Brown and Zunker, 1966). Thus, although the percentage of institutions reporting that they used students in helping roles remained relatively stable over the eight years between the two reports, the types of activities that students performed had expanded.

Zunker (1975) conducted a follow-up study in spring 1974 and concluded that the number of student paraprofessional programs had increased in the ten years since the study by Brown and Zunker (1966). Of the 220 responding institutions, 76 percent reported that they used student counselors in student affairs programs. Although use of student paraprofessionals remained quite high in residence halls and orientation programs (90 percent and 87 percent respectively), the practice was increasing in academic departments (24 percent), reading and study habits centers (22 percent), and counseling centers (29 percent). Increasingly, students were also helping students in the areas of student activities (21 percent) and student religious centers (16 percent).

Zunker (1975) found no significant changes in the procedures used to select student paraprofessionals from those reported by Brown and Zunker (1966) or by Powell (1959). Programs continued to use the criteria reported by Powell: leadership experience, grades, and faculty and staff recommendations. Zunker (1975) concluded that training for student paraprofessionals had remained rather haphazard.

Salovey (1983) and Ender and Winston (1984) conducted independent studies at the same time. Salovey (1983) polled 200 counseling center directors. Of the 156 respondents, 78 percent said that their campus had an active peer counseling program.

Ender and Winston (1984) surveyed 200 chief student affairs administrators selected at random from *Peterson's Annual Guide to Undergraduate Study* (1983). Responses were received from 118 institutions. Eighty-five institutions (72 percent) reported having one or more undergraduate paraprofessional programs on their campus. In all, the chief student affairs administrators reported 409 active paraprofessional programs. The same authors also polled paraprofessional program coordinators at the institutions in their survey and received responses from 237 paraprofessional program coordinators, representing 58 percent of the programs identified by the survey.

Comparing the results of the two most recent studies, it appears that between 72 percent and 78 percent of all student affairs divisions in higher education use student paraprofessionals as undergraduate counselors. These figures indicate no substantial shift in the percentage of utilization noted by Zunker (1975). However, the number of program settings in which student paraprofessionals were used had increased. Table 1 displays the percentage

Table 1. Utilization of Paraprofessionals in Student Affairs (N = 85)

Program Type	Rank	N	% of N
Student orientation	1	70	82.4
Residence halls	2	69	81.2
Student judiciary/discipline	3	47	55.3
Student activities/union	4	46	54.1
Counseling center	5	29	34.5
Career planning/placement	6.5	28	32.9
Academic advising	6.5	28	32.9
Religious centers	8.5	17	20.0
Crisis intervention	8.5	17	20.0
Financial aid	10	16	18.8
Study skills/tutorial[a]	11	15	18.0
International student programs	12	13	15.3
Research and evaluation	13.5	7	8.2
Other	13.5	7	8.2

[a]Data were requested only from student affairs programs; consequently, study skills/tutorial programs are underrepresented, since many are housed in academic affairs.

Source: Ender and Winston, 1984.

of student affairs settings that are now using student paraprofessionals. In the study on which Table 1 is based (Ender and Winston, 1984, p. 1), paraprofessionals were defined as "undergraduate students who have been selected and trained to offer services or programs to their peers. These services are intentionally designed to assist in the adjustment, satisfaction, and/or persistence of students as applied to the educational experience."

As Table 1 shows, student paraprofessionals are still heavily employed in student orientation programs (82 percent) and in residence hall settings (81 percent). Utilization seems to be increasing in student judiciary programs (55 percent), student activities (54 percent), counseling centers (35 percent)— Salovey (1983) reports 34 percent utilization in this area—career planning (33 percent)—Salovey (1983) reports 35 percent utilization in this area—academic advising (32.9 percent), religious centers (20 percent), and crisis intervention programs (20 percent). The percentage in study skills/tutorial programs (18 percent) is quite low and seemingly suspect. This low figure may be explained in part by the fact that the survey was sent to student affairs vice-presidents; many study skills/tutorial programs are located in academic departments and divisions.

Why the Increased Utilization?

Several factors help to explain the increased utilization of paraprofessionals in student affairs divisions: Research supports the effectiveness of student paraprofessionals. Service in a paraprofessional position has a positive impact on the growth and development of students. Use of paraprofessionals enables institutions to offer more services and programs to students on campus. Paraprofessional-staffed programs are less expensive than professional-staffed programs, and use of paraprofessionals enables professionals' time to be used to provide services more in line with their educational background and expertise. Finally, service as paraprofessional is becoming part of the educational program requirements on many campuses.

Paraprofessional Effectiveness. A number of writers (Brown, 1974; Delworth and others, 1974; Ender and McFadden, 1980) have argued the effectiveness of paraprofessionals by citing research (Carkhuff, 1968, 1969; Carkhuff and Truax, 1965; Zunker and Brown, 1966; Brown and others, 1971). Carkhuff and Truax (1965) found that paraprofessionals were only slightly less effective than professionals in providing therapeutic assistance in mental health settings. Zunker and Brown (1966) concluded that paraprofessional counselors were as effective as professional counselors in providing academic adjustment assistance to entering freshmen.

Other studies find that students who receive academic advising from other students have more positive attitudes toward their advisors and lower dropout rates than students advised by faculty (Brown and Myers, 1975). Barrow and Hetherington (1981) compared the effectiveness of student-trained paraprofessionals with that of professionals in leading social anxiety management groups and found that subjects in both groups improved significantly. There was no evidence that the groups led by professionals and by paraprofessionals differed in the amount of decrease in social anxiety, and there were no major differences in rates of participation or attrition.

Getz and Miles (1978) looked at student preferences for service providers by comparing four groups—male professional counselors, female professional counselors, male peer counselors, and female peer counselors. The results of their study indicated that students preferred assistance from student counselors in the area of drug-related concerns, while there was a slight preference among both sexes for peer counselors in the area of adjustment to self and others. However, there was an overall preference for professional counselors. This finding suggests that peer counselors will never take the place of professionals as overall service providers within a counseling center but that they can specialize in certain areas, such as drug-related concerns and self-adjustment, if they have the approval and acceptance of students seeking services.

Ender and Winston (1984) gathered information about the rationales for paraprofessional helpers as determined by paraprofessional program directors and coordinators. Of the 237 respondents, 51 percent said that one rationale for using students in paraprofessional roles was that students could be more effective than professionals in assisting students with their normal developmental concerns.

Impact on Paraprofessionals. The reason for utilizing paraprofessionals in departments of student affairs that program coordinators ranked first was the impact that it had on the student paraprofessionals themselves (Ender and Winston, 1984). Of the 237 respondents, 67 percent indicated that that was one of their reasons for establishing paraprofessional-staffed programs. Ender (1983) has advocated the intentional structuring of programs in ways that will capitalize on the developmental dynamics occurring through this staffing technique. Heath (1980) has pointed out that the personal development of college students can be enhanced through programs that expect and encourage students to take responsibility for the growth of others and that provide students with opportunities to assume alternative roles. These principles can be actualized when a paraprofessional-staffed program is implemented.

Increased Services at Reduced Cost. Sixty-two percent of the respondents to the survey by Ender and Winston (1984) said that student-staffed programs allowed institutions to offer more services, and 50 percent said that student-staffed programs made services less costly.

It is important to note the types of services that are being offered. Table 2 lists the types of service offered by paraprofessionals, how these services were ranked by the 237 survey respondents, and the percentages of the various types of paraprofessional programs in which these activities figure. The top six activities are clearly developmental in nature, and they do not require professionals as the primary service providers. Important tasks that seem routine to professionals—providing information, explaining institutional and program policies, and performing clerical tasks—can be performed by paraprofessionals, who consider their responsibilities in these areas exciting, stimulating, and helpful. The high activity rate for providing referral information seems to indicate that professionals can use their time more effectively by assisting the students whose concerns exceed the paraprofessionals' expertise. It is worthy to note that 54 percent of the survey respondents used paraprofessionals in counseling-type activities. This indicates that paraprofessionals are assisting their peers in a way that has been generally regarded as a professional activity.

Freeing Professional Time. Professional time can be used more wisely thanks to paraprofessional helpers. Not only can more students be served, but professionals can use their expertise more fully in assisting referred students and in training and supervising the working paraprofessionals. In many program areas that address primarily developmental needs, the impact of one professional who supervises five paraprofessionals as they assist fifty students during the work day seems to have several advantages for cost-effectiveness and utilization of professional expertise.

Paraprofessionals and Educational Programming. Student affairs professionals continue to lobby and seek involvement with their colleagues among the faculty. A symbiotic relationship can be developed through the interaction of paraprofessional programming and academic curriculums. Of the 237 program coordinators who responded to Ender and Winston (1984), fifty (22 percent) said that paraprofessional programs were part of the para-

Table 2. Work Activity, Percentage of Agreement: Composite Findings and Work Settings

Activity	Rank	Composite Programs n = 237	Residence Halls n = 65	Counseling/Career Centers n = 23	Orientation n = 30	Advising n = 9	Student Activities n = 17	Student Judiciary n = 18	Study Skills n = 15	Other n = 60
Providing information	1	92%	98% (65)	100% (96)	100% (90)	100% (89)	82% (59)	61% (56)	73% (53)	92% (55)
Explaining policies and procedures	2	79	98 (71)	65 (26)	83 (63)	100 (67)	65 (29)	56 (50)	40 (33)	80 (68)
Performing administrative and clerical tasks	3	68	85 (34)	65 (48)	60 (40)	56 (22)	71 (65)	22 (17)	47 (33)	73 (55)
Making referrals	4	60	88 (31)	52 (39)	60 (37)	100 (89)	35 (12)	33 (22)	27 (20)	50 (27)
Counseling	5.5	54	92 (66)	48 (39)	43 (37)	56 (33)	29 (12)	22 (17)	20 (01)	45 (00)
Implementing social activities	5.5	54	92 (52)	13 (00)	70 (47)	67 (33)	88 (71)	01 (00)	13 (01)	33 (00)
Enforcing rules	7	48	92 (75)	00 (00)	20 (00)	22 (11)	53 (35)	78 (72)	00 (00)	35 (30)
Collecting data	8	46	54 (00)	70 (35)	43 (27)	11 (00)	29 (01)	17 (11)	33 (27)	50 (30)
Academic advising	9	43	69 (09)	61 (35)	50 (23)	89 (78)	01 (01)	00 (00)	33 (27)	22 (18)
Facilitating community development	10	37	72 (47)	00 (00)	40 (27)	44 (22)	53 (29)	11 (11)	00 (00)	18 (12)
Assisting with study skills	11	33	62 (00)	35 (22)	13 (00)	78 (11)	00 (00)	00 (00)	01 (73)	13 (00)
Providing crisis intervention	12	32	72 (23)	26 (17)	10 (00)	33 (11)	18 (01)	11 (00)	13 (01)	15 (13)
Teaching and tutoring	13	18	17 (00)	26 (13)	00 (00)	56 (11)	12 (12)	01 (01)	87 (87)	01 (00)
Interpreting test results	14	09	00 (00)	30 (17)	13 (00)	22 (22)	01 (01)	00 (00)	01 (01)	01 (00)

Note: Numbers in parentheses represent the percentage of programs indicating that an activity was among the top five functions performed by paraprofessionals.

Source: Ender and Winston, 1984.

professionals educational program. Working as a paraprofessional can serve to establish students' professional interests and aptitudes in many professional areas, such as teacher education, social work, psychology, and child and family development. The results of the Ender and Winston survey indicate that many colleges are realizing this possibility.

Student Paraprofessionals: A Definition

Perhaps one of the major shortcomings in the development of paraprofessional programs across the country is the absence of a clear definition. Paraprofessionals have been referred to as *student counselors, student helpers, student paraprofessional helpers, student assistants,* and *student aides.* The absence of either a term or a definition that cuts across program settings has affected the generalizability of research studies, training procedures, and the image of what student paraprofessionals can do.

The issue of language consistency within the profession of student affairs was a matter of great concern for many years (Crookston, 1976). The field grappled with such terms as *student personnel, student affairs, student services,* and *student development.* Just as professional identification and purpose has been unclear, so has the issue of paraprofessional identification and purpose. Ender (1983, p. 324) has proposed a definition that seems to encompass the definitions offered by Delworth and Aulepp (1976), Delworth and others (1974), Brown (1977), and Ender and others (1979): "Paraprofessionals are students who have been selected and trained to offer educational services to their peers. These services are intentionally designed to assist in the adjustment, satisfaction, and persistence of students toward attainment of their educational goals. Students performing in paraprofessional roles are compensated for their services and supervised by qualified professionals."

The terms *adjustment, satisfaction,* and *persistence* help the definition to focus on the developmental nature of the paraprofessional's role as a helper within higher education. Paraprofessional helpers fulfill such functions as assisting, teaching, and supporting; they do not remediate, train, or interpret (Ender and others, 1981). Figure 1 relates the developmental nature of the paraprofessional's role to issues outside the paraprofessional's realm of expertise.

There is overlap between the various types of student concerns and who is best suited to address the issues involved. The amount and degree of training provided to paraprofessionals and the availability of supervision help to answer this question. The ability to assess students' concerns and to make timely referrals is of paramount importance if the paraprofessional is to be viable in his or her helping role. Student paraprofessional helpers must be in a position to help students assess the degree of psychological dissonance associated with their problem or concern. A problem associated with the developmental end of the continuum shown in Figure 1 is probably not

Figure 1. Student Concerns and Sources of Help Breadth of Concerns/Problems Presented by Students

Program Setting	Paraprofessional Intervention	Possible Referral Area	Professional Intervention Required
	Development in Nature		*Therapeutic, Remedial, or Needing Professional Expertise*
Residence Halls	Student is unsure of how to get involved in campus activities.	Student is anxious but energetic about meeting new people.	Student is paranoid, depressed, and frightened about involvement with others.
Counseling Center	Student has educational needs pertaining to birth control.	Student is unsure about using birth control and feels pressured by partner.	Student is pregnant and frightened about possible outcome with boyfriend, friends, and family.
Career Center	Freshman student wants to explore and read vocational material.	Student is unsure about two vocational areas and needs to make choice.	Student has no idea about his or her interests, attitudes, and aptitudes concerning vocational interests and choices.
Study Skills Lab	Student wants tutor in math.	Student likes math but does not get along with math teacher.	Student experiences extreme anxiety when taking math tests.
Orientation	Student desires tour of design studio.	Student wants explanation of design curriculum.	Student wants portfolio assessed to determine whether he or she is eligible for design major.
Academic Advising	Student needs to know prerequisites for Eng. 220.	Student wants to assess background and readiness to enroll in Eng. 220.	Physics major wants to know why Eng. 220 is required for major. He or she is angry and frustrated due to poor performance in course.

Source: Ender and Winston, 1982.

overwhelming, and there is only a little stress, so that the student's needs can be met by information.

In the center of the continuum, the paraprofessional may help by providing the student with an opportunity to enter into more of a helping relationship. The psychological dissonance and corresponding stress are greater here. In this context, the paraprofessional makes use of appropriate listening and relationship skills.

When student concerns are associated with the right side of the continuum, the paraprofessional should strive to make a timely and appropriate referral. Many times, students who have problems in this area are also overwhelmed, frightened, and experiencing great stress. These concerns must be addressed by a professional helper. Paraprofessionals should never feel the types of responsibility associated with being a professional. Student paraprofessionals should not be put in the position of having to worry that they are responsible for students or their concerns after they leave the program setting at the end of the workday. Such worry is to be felt only by qualified professionals.

Need For Standards

The development of an acceptable statement of standards to guide professionals as they plan and implement paraprofessional programs could be a major step forward in student paraprofessional programs. Mable and Miller (1983) argue for the necessity of standards in the student affairs professional—both work activity and training—and many of their reasons seem appropriate. According to these authors, standards serve as uniform reference points as student affairs practitioners and institutional leaders evaluate the quality of student service programs, evaluate staff members, and give direction for creating new and better programs of intentional development. Moreover, standards help to assure higher-quality staff and programs and they help to assure higher-quality experiences for students receiving program services. Finally, standards provide consistent criteria for institutional and academic accreditation.

At present, there is no uniform set of standards to guide practitioners as they develop and maintain paraprofessional programs. The absence of such standards has led to a certain ambiguity within the student paraprofessional movement. However, an attempt has been made to formulate standards for the purpose of defining minimal expectations of a student paraprofessional program (Ender and others, 1981). These proposed standards were developed and written within the guidelines and for the areas defined by the Council for the Advancement of Standards for Student Services/Development Programs (CAS). At present, eighteen professional associations, which represent various interests of student affairs practice and preparation programs, belong to the CAS (Mable and Miller, 1983).

The proposed standards can be found in Appendix B of this volume. They address ten areas associated with paraprofessional programs: purpose and goals, human resources, programs/services/activities, facilities, financial and other resources, relationships with faculty and other groups and agencies, planning, evaluation, ethics, and legal issues. For each area, there are minimal guidelines that a professional should address when designing and implementing a paraprofessional program, and for each standard, there is a corresponding interpretive statement that serves to illustrate and explicate it.

Several points need consideration as readers review Appendix B. First, the standards are presented as an example of what future recognized standards might entail and encompass. Second, they are presented in hopes of generating reaction, support, and professional debate about the viability of developing a standards statement that can guide paraprofessional practice and programming. Third, the standards were developed for possible CAS endorsement; however, this endorsement has yet to be given. The CAS has chosen not to address paraprofessional standards per se but rather to include a statement on use of paraprofessionals in the general guidelines now being developed by the council to guide student affairs practice in general (Miller, 1984). Given the broad base of paraprofessional programming within divisions of student affairs—between 72 and 78 percent of all divisions use student paraprofessionals—a general statement does not seem to address either the present scale of the practice or the need for consistency across programming areas. The reader is encouraged to enter the debate. Is a statement of standards to guide paraprofessional programming needed? Perhaps such a debate will prompt the CAS to definitive action as it continues to develop and approve standard statements to promote professionalism within student affairs.

Implementation of Paraprofessional Programming

Many writers have articulated models to guide the development of paraprofessional programs (Brown, 1977; Delworth and Aulepp, 1976; Delworth and others, 1974; Ender, 1983; Ender and McFadden, 1980; Ender and others, 1981; Sherwood, 1980; Upcraft and Pilato, 1982). These models consistently recognize eight program areas: program goals and objectives, recruitment, selection, training, supervision, compensation, evaluation, and ethical and legal issues. This section addresses these areas from a broad perspective that is applicable to all paraprofessional programs. It also discusses research by Ender and Winston (1984).

Program Goals and Objectives. Program goals and objectives should be established, written in behavioral terms, and disseminated to individuals on campus who are affected by the program intervention. Program goals should address the developmental needs of students that paraprofessional intervention can satisfy. Ender and Winston (1984) found that a majority of programs had both written job descriptions (79 percent) and program goals and objectives (64 percent). Programs that have not attended to these basic programming responsibilities are remiss. Without such statements, ambiguity and confusion can overwhelm both the paraprofessionals and students seeking their services.

Recruitment. The recruitment of student paraprofessionals is a critical area if programs are to attract students who have a genuine and sincere interest in assisting their peers. No matter what the technique, the primary purpose of recruitment is to establish a large pool of applicants who possess the human helping qualities of objectivity, honesty, capacity for relatedness, emotional security, integrity, patience, commitment to the helping process, and ability to demonstrate empathy (Parlott and others, 1978). In an attempt to recruit students who possess these qualities, programs generally use announcements, faculty, staff, and peer referrals, and word of mouth. Once recruited, students are generally asked to submit information to support their candidacy. Such materials include formal application forms (71 percent), letters of reference (38 percent), written essays describing why recruits would like to be a helper (19 percent), formal resumes (11 percent), and material gleaned from academic transcripts (9 percent) (Ender and Winston, 1984).

Selection Criteria and Processes. Program administrators advocate nine criteria for the selection process. In order, these criteria are: previous leadership experience (78 percent), recommendations from faculty and staff (73 percent), grades (63 percent), peer ratings (47 percent), performance in a training program (31 percent), academic major or field of academic study (22 percent), personality assessment instruments (15 percent), successful apprenticeship in the program (14 percent), and academic abilities tests (14 percent) (Ender and Winston, 1984). (The percentages add up to more than 100 percent because survey respondents were asked to list all criteria used in the selection process at their institution.) The criteria used are generally supported by the literature on student paraprofessionals and by the proposed standards statement.

Two other points concerning selection need to be raised. Writers who belong to the humanist and existential schools (Jung, 1964)—that is, not to the classical psychoanalytic or behavioral schools—think that the helper's personality is a significant criterion for the helper's effectiveness in helping interventions. Given that the training of most paraprofessionals emphasizes relationship skills, the use of personality assessment instruments as a selection device appears to have some merit. The Ender and Winston (1984) survey found very little attention given to this procedure (15 percent), which may be useful and which needs further investigation. Also, many authors advocate training prior to selection (Ender and McFadden, 1980; Ender, 1983; Upcraft and Pilato, 1982; Winston and Buckner, in press). In fact, Upcraft and others (1982, p. 37) compared resident assistants who were trained prior to final selection with resident assistants who had no preemployment training and found that "on every criteria (availability, approachability, information and referral, student conduct, floor atmosphere, and programming) the job performance of resident assistants who participated in the training was significantly better than that of the nontrained resident assistants." Winston and Buckner (in press) concluded that resident assistants trained prior to final selection and employment experienced less stress on the job than did their contemporaries who were trained while on the job. Research needs to be conducted in other types of paraprofessional programs to determine the generalizability of these findings. It is worthwhile to repeat that 31 percent of those who responded to the survey by Ender and Winston (1984) used performance in training as a final selection criterion. The proposed standards also encourage program directors to make training part of the selection process. One would not think of hiring professionals who had not been through a formal preparation program. Why should paraprofessionals not also receive pre-employment training?

The findings of Ender and Winston (1984) indicate that the selection procedures used in paraprofessional programs are still dominated by the individual interview (87 percent), followed by group interviews (46 percent) and both individual and group interviews (10 percent). Again, survey respondents were asked to indicate all applicable procedures. Role playing or simulations were used by 21 percent of the respondents as a selection procedure.

Training. At its best, training involves both pretraining and in-service training. At the minimum, such training should involve both generalist or core helping and job-specific skills (Delworth and others, 1974; Ender and McFadden, 1980). The initial preservice training provides the background and skills necessary to be a successful helper. The in-service training focuses on getting the job done. The minimum content areas for pretraining are described in the proposed standards statement. They include knowledge of the paraprofessional's role, awareness of self and the power associated with being a role model, community (support) skills, student development theory, communication and relationship skills, goal-setting and assessment techniques, campus resources and referral techniques, and cross-cultural relations. In-service training focuses on such areas as division goals and objectives; policies and procedures; ethical concerns, such as confidentiality; and job-specific knowledge and skills (Delworth and Yarris, 1978).

Perhaps the greatest disservice to student paraprofessionals and students receiving services is done in allowing too little time for the training experience. Zunker (1975) concluded that training for paraprofessionals was quite haphazard—a finding consistent with earlier studies. Table 3 illustrates the amount of training time devoted to preparation of new paraprofessionals in 235 programs. Twenty-nine percent of the polled programs reported less than five hours of training. However, 45 percent of the programs reported 16 hours or more of training, and this is encouraging. The greatest amount of training time appears to be occurring in residence halls and counseling settings. This writer would advocate a minimum of forty hours of preparation time in the core helping skills if interpersonal effectiveness is to be realized. Moreover, training should occur before employment begins. Sixty-two percent of the respondents to the Ender and Winston (1984) survey reported some type of training prior to beginning the job. While the time devoted to training is still insufficient, the fact that the majority of paraprofessional programs are providing some kind of training before the students begin work is encouraging.

Publications devoted to paraprofessional training have proliferated in the last five years—a broad leap forward for student paraprofessional training. These publications include texts for general training (Ender and others, 1979; D'Andrea and Salovey, 1983); texts for resident assistant training (Upcraft and others, 1982; Blimling and Miltenberger, 1981); and texts for training peer tutors (Arkin and Shollar, 1982).

However, textbooks are not widely used in the training experience. Of the 237 respondents to the survey by Ender and Winston (1984), only 16 percent indicated that a textbook was used. The majority of use occurred in resident assistant training (26 percent) and in training for work in counseling and career centers (30 percent). Although they are not widely used at this time, textbooks do have potential for providing training for student paraprofessional helpers with some degree of consistency. They all promote the importance of developing relationship skills in the training experience. Three of the five emphasize the importance of the acquisition of knowledge about student growth and development. Several address the core training areas proposed in the standards statement.

Supervision. Supervision is a necessary and essential component of paraprofessional programming. The supervisor has three primary roles in the supervisory relationship; consultation, teaching, and mentoring (Ender, 1983). In the consultant role, supervisors work closely with paraprofessionals to identify intervention strategies and cases that need referral. In the teaching role, supervisors provide additional training opportunities that address and reinforce helping skills covered in preservice training or that develop skills identified as necessary through program assessment and evaluation. In the mentoring role, supervisors model the helping skills that they expect paraprofessionals to provide. Supervisors are role models. They should exemplify the types of helping behaviors that they expect of paraprofessionals. Supervisors should demonstrate high energy levels as they engage with the program and with paraprofessionals.

Ender and Winston (1984) found that many paraprofessional programs used supervision activities. Of the 235 respondents, 90 percent indicated that supervision opportunities were available. More than 65 percent of the programs that offered supervision did so on at least a weekly basis, and

Table 3. Hours of Training Provided to New Paraprofessionals

Program Type	No Formal Training		5 Hours or Less		6–15 Hours		16–35 Hours		36–50 Hours		More Than 50 Hours	
	N	% of N	N	% of N	N	% of N	N	% of N	N	% of N	N	% of N
Composite (N = 235)	17	7.2	51	21.7	61	26.0	43	18.3	29	12.3	34	14.5
Residence Halls (N = 64)	2	3.1	1	1.6	8	12.5	15	23.4	20	31.3	18	28.1
Counseling and Career Centers (N = 23)	1	4.3	1	4.3	8	34.8	5	21.7	2	8.7	6	26.1
Orientation (N = 30)	1	3.3	9	30.0	11	36.7	5	16.7	2	6.7	2	6.7
Advising (N = 9)	0	0.0	2	22.2	3	33.3	3	33.3	0	0.0	1	11.1
Student Activities (N = 17)	2	11.8	6	35.3	4	23.5	3	17.6	1	5.9	1	5.9
Student Judiciary (N = 18)	3	16.7	6	33.3	6	33.3	2	11.1	1	5.6	0	0.0
Study Skills (N = 15)	2	13.3	6	40.0	5	33.3	2	13.3	0	0.0	0	0.0
Other (N = 59)	6	10.2	20	33.9	16	27.1	8	13.6	3	5.1	6	10.2

Source: Ender and Winston, 1984.

eighty-nine programs (48 percent) offered supervision on a daily basis. This finding is reassuring, because supervision is a major key to program success.

Compensation. In more than three-fourths (76.9 percent) of the programs surveyed by Ender and Winston (1984), paraprofessionals received compensation. The most preferred method of compensation was monetary (57 percent), followed by in-kind support (21 percent). Types of in-kind support included room, board, and tuition waiver. Fifty-four programs (23 percent) provided no compensation. Presumably, these programs used paraprofessionals on a voluntary basis. Most writers on the use of paraprofessionals advocate tangible compensation for the services provided by paraprofessionals, as does the proposed standard statement.

Evaluation. Evaluation of paraprofessional programs is critical. One of the most disheartening findings of the study by Ender and Winston (1984) was that 45 percent of the programs surveyed lacked evaluation procedures. This seems to suggest a weak link in paraprofessional administration—one that must be overcome if the potential of such programming efforts is to be realized. If evaluation is not occurring, one might suspect an absence of clear-cut, measurable program objectives. The absence of evaluation may also help to explain why there is not more research literature on the effectiveness of paraprofessionals in student affairs settings. The proposed standard statement clearly advocates the evaluation phase of program management and administration.

Legal and Ethical Issues. The ethical issues pertaining to paraprofessional programming are detailed in Section Nine of Appendix B. Primarily, paraprofessionals should adhere to the ethical guidelines that prevail for the service area. These ethical concerns should be addressed both in training and during supervision. Respondents to the Ender and Winston (1984) survey indicated that only seventy-five programs (32 percent) had developed a statement of ethical guidelines. This area needs more attention if paraprofessionals' credibility and effectiveness are to be assured.

Legally, there are many grey areas in student paraprofessionalism. At the very least, the sponsoring agency should be legally liable for the services provided by paraprofessionals. This point deserves more than passing notice. Clearly stated paraprofessional role definitions and clear-cut program objectives should be scrutinized for legal implications.

The Future of Student Paraprofessional Programming

Delworth (1974) stated that paraprofessionals were not only coming but in fact were already here. Ten years later, use of paraprofessionals seems to be well entrenched in student affairs settings and agencies. Coordinators of paraprofessional programs in divisions of student affairs are moving to upgrade the status of student paraprofessional helpers. This movement is welcomed, encouraged, and supported. The increased utilization of paraprofessionals across broad areas of student affairs, the appearance of training manuals, and the proposed statement of standards to govern paraprofessional programs all point to increased action and interest within the paraprofessional movement.

Chief administrators in divisions of student affairs are optimistic about the future of student paraprofessionalism. Of the administrators surveyed by Ender and Winston (1984), forty-nine of the eighty-five (58 percent) who indicated that there was paraprofessional programming on their campus expected the number of paraprofessionals to increase during the next ten years. Mable and DeCoster (1981) encourage the expansion of student services and developmental programs through greater involvement of students as paraprofessionals, peer counselors, advisors, and college leaders. An institution's most valuable resource is its students. Finding avenues to promote students' developmental growth is a responsibility and duty for all those involved in student affairs. The development, expansion, and maintenance of programs staffed by student paraprofessionals shows that this is an excellent method of upholding this responsibility.

References

Arkin, M., and Shollar, B. *The Tutor Book.* New York: Longman, 1982.

Barrow, J., and Hetherington, C. "Training Paraprofessionals to Lead Social Anxiety Management Groups." *Journal of College Student Personnel,* 1981, *22* (3), 269–273.

Blimling, G. S., and Miltenberger, L. J. *The Resident Assistant: Working With College Students in Residence Halls.* Dubuque, Iowa: Kendall/Hunt, 1981.

Brown, W. F. "Effectiveness of Paraprofessionals: The Evidence." *Personnel and Guidance Journal,* 1974, *53* (4), 257–263.

Brown, W. F. *Student-to-Student Counseling.* (Rev. ed.) Austin: University of Texas Press, 1977.

Brown, C. R., and Myers, R. "Student Versus Faculty Curriculum Advising." *Journal of College Student Personnel,* 1975, *16* (3), 226–231.

Brown, W. F., and Zunker, V. G. "Student Counselor Utilization at Four-Year Institutions of Higher Learning." *Journal of College Student Personnel,* 1966, *7,* 41–46.

Brown, W. F., Wehe, N. O., Haslam, W. L., and Zunker, V. G. "Effectiveness of Student-to-Student Counseling on the Academic Adjustment of Potential College Dropouts." *Journal of Educational Psychology,* 1971, *64,* 285–289.

Carkhuff, R. R. "Differential Functioning of Lay and Professional Helpers." *Journal of Counseling Psychology,* 1968, *15,* 117–126.

Carkhuff, R. R. *Helping and Human Relations.* New York: Holt, Rinehart and Winston, 1969.

Carkhuff, R. R., and Truax, C. B. "Lay Mental Health Counseling: The Effects of Lay Group Counseling." *Journal of Counseling Psychology,* 1965, *29,* 426–431.

Crookston, B. "Student Personnel—All Hail and Farewell!" *Personnel and Guidance Journal,* 1976, *55* (1), 26–29.

D'Andrea, V., and Salovey, P. *Peer Counseling: Skills and Perspectives.* Palo Alto, Calif.: Science and Behavior Books, 1983.

Delworth, U. "The Paraprofessionals are Coming!" *Personnel and Guidance Journal,* 1974, *53* (4), 250.

Delworth, U., and Aulepp, L. *Training Manual for Paraprofessionals and Allied Professional Programs.* Boulder, Colo.: Western Interstate Commission for Higher Education, 1976.

Delworth, U., and Yarris, E. "Concepts and Processes for the New Training Role." In U. Delworth (Ed.), *Training Competent Staff.* New Directions for Student Services, no. 2. San Francisco: Jossey-Bass, 1978.

Delworth, U., Sherwood, G., and Casaburri, N. *Student Paraprofessionals: A Working Model for Higher Education.* Washington, D.C.: American College Personnel Association, 1974.

Ender, S. C. "Students as Paraprofessionals." In T. K. Miller, R. B. Winston, Jr., and W. R. Mendenhall (Eds.), *Administration and Leadership in Student Affairs: Actualizing Student Development in Higher Education.* Muncie, Ind.: Accelerated Development, 1983.

Ender, S. C., and McFadden, R. "Training the Student Paraprofessional Helper." In F. B. Newton and K. L. Ender (Eds.), *Student Development Practices: Strategies for Making a Difference.* Springfield, Ill.: Thomas, 1980.

Ender, S. C., and Winston, R. B., Jr. "Training Allied Professional Academic Advisors." In R. B. Winston, Jr., S. C. Ender, and T. K. Miller (Eds.), *Developmental Approaches to Academic Advising.* New Directions for Student Services, no. 17. San Francisco: Jossey-Bass, 1982.

Ender, S. C., and Winston, R. B., Jr. "A National Survey of Student Paraprofessional Utilization in Student Affairs." Unpublished manuscript, Kansas State University, 1984.

Ender, S. C., McCaffrey, S. S., and Miller, T. K. *Students Helping Students: A Training Manual for Peer Helpers on the College Campus.* Athens, Ga.: Student Development Associates, 1979.

Ender, S. C., Schuette, C. G., and Neuberger, C. G. "Proposed Standards for Students Serving as Paraprofessionals: Employment and Utilization." Unpublished document, Kansas State University and The American University, 1981.

Getz, H. G., and Miles, J. H. "Women and Peers as Counselors." *Journal of College Student Personnel,* 1978, *19* (1), 37–41.

Heath, P. H. "Wanted: A Comprehensive Model of Healthy Development." *The Personnel and Guidance Journal,* 1980, *58* (5), 391–399.

Hegener, K. C., Hunter, J., and Kaye, C. (Eds.), *Peterson's Annual Guide to Undergraduate Study,* 1983 edition. Princeton, N.J.: Peterson's Guides, 1982.

Jung, C. G. "The State of Psychotherapy Today (1934)." In *Collected Works. Vol. 10: Civilization in Transition.* Princeton, N.J.: Princeton University Press, 1964.

Mable, P., and DeCoster, D. A. "Postsecondary Education Futures: Implications, Innovations, and Initiatives." In D. A. DeCoster and P. Mable (Eds.), *Understanding Today's Students.* New Directions for Student Services, no. 16. San Francisco: Jossey-Bass, 1981.

Mable, P., and Miller, T. K. "Standards for Professional Practice." In T. K. Miller, R. B. Winston, Jr., and W. R. Mendenhall (Eds.), *Administration and Leadership in Student Affairs: Actualizing Student Development in Higher Education.* Muncie, Ind.: Accelerated Development, 1983.

Miller, T. K. Personal communication, January 1984.

Parlott, M. B., Waskow, I. E., and Wolfe, B. E. "Research on Therapist Variables in Relation to Process and Outcome." In S. L. Garfield and A. E. Bergin (Eds.), *Handbook of Psychotherapy and Behavior Change.* (2nd ed.) New York: Wiley, 1978.

Powell, O. B. "The Student Who Assumes Counseling Responsibilities." In M. D. Hardee (Ed.), *The Faculty in College Counseling.* New York: McGraw-Hill, 1959.

Powell, J. R., Pyler, S. A., Dickerson, B.A., and McClellan, S. D. *The Personnel Assistant in College Resident Halls.* New York: Houghton Mifflin, 1969.

Salovey, P. "A Survey of Campus Peer Counseling Activities." Paper presented at a meeting of the American College Health Association, St. Louis, May 1983.

Sherwood, G. P. "Allied and Paraprofessional Assistance." In U. Delworth, G. R. Hanson, and Associates (Eds.), *Student Services: A Handbook for the Profession.* San Francisco: Jossey-Bass, 1981.

Upcraft, M. L., and Pilato, G. T. *Residence Hall Assistants in College: A Guide to Selection, Training, and Supervision.* San Francisco: Jossey-Bass, 1982.

Upcraft, M. L., Pilato, G. T., and Peterman, D. J. *Learning to be a Resident Assistant: A Manual for Effective Participation in the Training Program.* San Francisco: Jossey-Bass, 1982.

Winston, R. B., and Buckner, J. D. "The Effects of Peer Helper Training and Timing of Training on Resident Assistants' Reported Stress." *Journal of College Student Personnel,* in press.

Zunker, V. G. "Students as Paraprofessionals in Four-Year Colleges and Universities." *Journal of College Student Personnel,* 1975, *16* (4), 282–286.

Zunker, V. G., and Brown, W. F. "Comparative Effectiveness of Student and Professional Counselors." *Personnel and Guidance Journal,* 1966, *44* (7), 738–743.

Steven C. Ender is assistant professor and counselor in the Center for Student Development at Kansas State University. Actively involved in paraprofessional programs throughout his professional career, he has coauthored a training manual for paraprofessionals, and he has been actively involved in training professionals who desire to implement paraprofessional programs.

Paraprofessionals have made a significant contribution to the
growth and expansion of learning assistance programs.

Student Paraprofessionals in the Learning Skills Center

Georgine Materniak

Of all paraprofessionals, the tutor can claim the oldest history and tradition in higher education. Formally or informally, students have always assisted and supported one another in academic endeavors. "Tutors have long been available in public colleges and universities, if a student could afford to hire them. . . . Tutoring has also been the way for poor students to work their way through college, while student members of honor societies, motivated by a sense of noblesse oblige, have a long history of offering free tutoring to their less academically successful peers" (Maxwell, 1979, p. 59).

The learning assistance movement emerged during the 1970s. In 1975, it was reported that, of all the existing learning centers, 53 percent had become operational since 1970 (Devirian and others, 1975). Dedicated to the academic success of students, learning centers made tutorial programs an integral part of learning assistance. Thus, one of the youngest units of higher education, the learning center, gave new life and meaning to the oldest paraprofessional role.

This chapter explores the role of student paraprofessionals in the learning center. First, the history of the relationship between learning assistance and paraprofessionalism is reviewed. Next, the needs and characteristics of students who use learning center services are described. This discussion in turn provides a basis for defining the roles and characteristics of para-

S. Ender, R. Winston (Eds.). *Using Students as Paraprofessional Staff.* New
Directions for Student Services, no. 27. San Francisco: Jossey-Bass, September 1984.

professionals in the learning center environment, and some suggestions for determining the differences between the duties of professionals and parapro- fessionals in learning centers are made. After addressing some of the mana- gerial and administrative issues raised by paraprofessional programs in learning centers, the chapter concludes with examples of some noteworthy peer learning assistance programs.

Learning Assistance and Paraprofessionals

A Brief History. The roots of the learning center can be traced to special programs created in the late 1960s to help nontraditional students make a positive academic, social, and cultural adjustment to college. In the early 1970s, these special programs, which often had tutorial components, were replaced or assimilated by comprehensive learning centers "due in part to the dismal failure of remedial and compensatory programs based on special classes" (Enright and Kerstiens, 1980, p. 8).

The emergence of comprehensive learning centers shifted the focus from remedial education, which emphasizes correcting the deficiencies of underprepared students, to developmental education—an approach based on the premise that all students should receive assistance to optimize their strengths as well as to overcome their weaknesses (Clowes, 1980; Cross, 1971). Learning centers were dedicated to helping all students maximize their full learning potential and become "more independent, self-confident, and efficient learners so that they will be better able to meet the university's academic standards and attain their own educational goals" (Maxwell, 1979, p. 112).

As the learning centers grew, increasing numbers of students made increasing demands for service. Often, there was little if any increase in budget and professional staff. Therefore, student tutors became a cost-effec- tive solution for expanding staff and services while freeing the time of professionals so that they could put their expertise to use where it was most needed. Tutors increased the time options for appointments, possessed knowledge about a vast assortment of academic subjects, and increased the opportunities for individualized instruction. In addition, the academically talented and successful students who acted as tutors helped to convince skeptical faculty of the importance of the learning center.

The heavy reliance of learning centers on student staff led to the formalization of peer programs, which had grown beyond the traditional realm of student volunteer services. Learning center professionals had to develop models and materials for selecting, training, supervising, and man- aging tutors and to define new peer roles, such as study skills counselors. This professional commitment to peer programs not only resulted in the para- professionalization of learning center student roles, but it also drew attention to the importance of other student roles on campus. There is no doubt that the increasing interest in paraprofessional programs witnessed over the past decade was largely influenced by the success of the mutually beneficial relationship that developed between learning services and student staff.

Student Needs and Characteristics. Because a comprehensive learning center takes a developmental perspective when helping students, it provides a broad range of services. Learning centers attract all segments of the student population—freshmen and graduate students, returning adults and students of traditional age, high-risk and honor students. The needs of such special groups as the handicapped, the learning-disabled, and international students also receive attention.

The needs of students who seek assistance center on two areas: learning skills and affective concerns. Learning skills include reading, writing, math, study skills, critical thinking, problem solving, reasoning, English as a second language, and subject matter tutoring. Affective concerns involved with learning include problems with anxiety (math, test, speech, writing), procrastination, motivation, self-concept, confidence, achievement, career decision, locus of control, persistence, organization, and time management.

Each of the learning skills and affective concerns can be placed on a continuum ranging from intense remediation to short-term developmental assistance. On the developmental end of the study skills continuum, we may find a first-term freshman who has done well in the past but who detects that studying for college is different from studying in previous environments. On the other end, we may find a sophomore who has been placed on academic probation because he or she lacks a disciplined approach to studying. The freshman's needs are a developmental skills concern. The sophomore requires remedial intervention in both the skills and the affective areas.

To accommodate this broad spectrum of needs, learning centers offer programs in a variety of formats, including group and individual instruction and self-paced lab programs. When the possible combinations of student needs and instructional formats are considered, it becomes apparent why learning centers are rich opportunities for paraprofessional roles.

Characteristics of Learning Center Paraprofessionals. Regardless of their specific functions, all learning center paraprofessional roles have three points in common. First, the peer must be knowledgeable about the subject matter, the peer must be able to explain and apply concepts, and the peer must have mastered the learning skills to be taught. Second, learning center paraprofessionals must model appropriate learning behaviors, attitudes, and strategies. It is essential for their words and actions to be congruent. Third, the paraprofessional is a facilitator of connections—helping a student to connect the use of new skills with everyday course work, helping a student to connect with options, alternatives, and resources, and helping a student to become more in tune with himself or herself.

Training will increase proficiency and skill, but a potential peer helper must already possess the three fundamental characteristics just outlined. By expressing content in an accurate and understandable manner, by modeling appropriate behavior and attitude, and by facilitating awareness and action in dealing with problems, the paraprofessional can help others to become confident and independent learners who take charge of their own academic destiny.

Given these three fundamental aspects of the role of the learning center paraprofessional, we can outline the basic qualities that one should expect from a learning center paraprofessional: a genuine concern for helping others in academic, social, and personal development; above-average intelligence, so that training and experience can be quickly assimilated; maturity, responsibility, and organization; good verbal and nonverbal inter-personal skills; the ability to accept and work with people of diverse back-grounds, beliefs, and values; the ability to define a problem and generate alternatives; self-confidence and good decision-making abilities; and a sense of humor (Johnson, 1981).

Paraprofessional Roles in Learning Skills Centers. A survey of college learning centers gathered some information about paraprofessional programs (Burlingame and others, 1982). Based on 153 responses, it was determined that paraprofessionals performed ten basic functions: tutoring (84 percent), staffing office or laboratory (70 percent), administering tests (40 percent), teaching workshops (38 percent), providing outreach programming (26 percent), co-teaching workshops (25 percent), conducting research (20 percent), assisting in program planning (19 percent), co-teaching classes (18 percent), and teaching classes (19 percent).

The high frequency with which paraprofessionals performed service activities (25 percent or above) is not surprising. Traditionally, students have tutored, provided assistance in learning labs, administered tests, and conducted workshops. However, the less frequent activities noted above occur in areas associated with such professional duties as teaching, conducting research, and planning programs. Does this mean that peers are cutting into professional territory? The more accurate interpretation is that low-frequency activities are indications of specialization of the paraprofessional role.

Professionals in learning centers recognized that the need for frequent training had to be reduced and that the continuity of peer staff had to increase. To accomplish these goals, they recruited students earlier in their college careers and expected them to make a commitment of two or more years. Students usually mastered the role for which they were trained within a year. After that, they automatically integrated individual talents, skills, and knowledge into their peer work and developed special interests and expertise. Discovering that bright and dedicated paraprofessionals could be groomed for more sophisticated roles, professionals took students under their charge and fostered their growth by giving them new and additional responsibilities.

The less-frequent activities reported in the survey are typical examples of paraprofessional specialization. They include outreach services, involvement in formal teaching environments, assisting professionals with research related to peer programs, revision of learning center curriculum and materials, and creation of new programs. In addition, some paraprofessionals have a special interest in working with specific student populations, such as international students, the handicapped, the learning-disabled, and returning adults. Those with organizational or managerial skills can be valuable in assisting with the day-to-day operations of peer programs by doing payroll, assigning rooms and schedules, and designing publicity. Other specializations include peer training and supervision. Experienced paraprofessionals are excellent resources for assistance with the recruitment, interviewing, and selection of candidates and for coaching and supporting peers in training.

A major concern about paraprofessionalism and peer specialization is that paraprofessional and professional roles can overlap. Table 1 distinguishes the duties of professionals and paraprofessionals in the learning center environment.

The basic duties of the learning center paraprofessional include assessing the student's needs, formulating a plan, providing instruction in content or skills and opportunities to practice the skills, evaluating the student's progress, and determining the student's future needs or goals. If difficulty arises in carrying out any phase of the duties and if the paraprofessional is certain that the difficulty is not due to a misunderstanding or error in judgment, professional intervention becomes necessary. Paraprofessionals should also learn to gauge the comfort level of interactions with peers. Any feelings of intimidation, manipulation, pressure, or anger that persist in an encounter indicate that professional involvement is required.

In addition to helping paraprofessionals become aware of the signs that signal their role boundaries, professionals have an obligation not to assign duties to paraprofessionals that are beyond their level of expertise and authority. For example, paraprofessionals who function as an integral part of an academic credit-bearing course should not be responsible for correcting work that will receive a grade or for presenting new material to students (Sexauer and Koloski, 1981). However, it is appropriate for the peer to collect and turn in homework or to review material that has already been presented in the class. For another example, peers and their clients must abide by the rules and regulations set forth by the professional, but it is not the peer's duty to administer punitive measures when clients violate the policy. Placing paraprofessionals in positions of expertise and authority defeats the purpose of having peer helpers. It destroys the nonjudgmental, nonthreatening, and supportive foundation that is a key to the peer relationship.

Responsible Behavior of Learning Center Paraprofessionals. The learning center paraprofessional must meet certain fundamental personal responsibilities: punctuality, attendance, participation in training, and receptivity

Table 1. Paraprofessionals and Professional Duties Within Learning Centers

Duties of a Learning Center Paraprofessional	Indication for Professional Intervention
Assessment	
Assess student needs:	
Administer and interpret diagnostic instruments relating to academic skill levels.	Assessment results are inconclusive, contradictory, or indicate a level of need above or below the range measured by the diagnostic instrument.
Interview the student.	
Observe a sample of the student's performance.	Student is resistive to or uncooperative in the assessment process.
Planning	
Formulate an appropriate and mutually agreeable plan for intervention.	Paraprofessional and student are unable to form and agree on an appropriate plan of intervention.
Instruction	
Present and demonstrate appropriate levels and usage of content or skills at a pace relevant to student's ability.	Student does not attend to or comprehend the content or demonstration presented by the paraprofessional.
	Student complains that instruction is not relevant, is too simple or complex, or is too fast or too slow.
Application	
Observe student's use of concepts and skills presented in the instructional phase.	Student is unable or unwilling to apply concepts or skills.
Evaluation	
Evaluate progress and provide feedback.	Progress is not made.
	Student is not receptive to evaluation or feedback.
Formulate a new plan or terminate the intervention.	Student denies the need for continued intervention or resists termination.

to supervision and evaluation. Peers must abide by office policy and procedures, model appropriate attitudes and behavior, make referrals when necessary, and maintain confidentiality. Therefore, it is absolutely essential for the director to state explicit rules of conduct and behavior. A few instances of irresponsible or unethical behavior and decisions by paraprofessionals can quickly destroy the credibility of an entire program.

Administrative and Managerial Concerns

Good management is the key to a successful paraprofessional program. Unless the learning center professional is committed to the recruitment, selection, training, supervision, and management of the peer program, it will fail, and that process itself can be quite destructive. The train them and leave them approach leads to certain failure. Paraprofessional programs require a continuous investment of professionals' time and effort. Successful programs are dynamic. New issues, concerns, and needs constantly arise. It is imperative for the professional to remain on top of day-to-day operations, keeping close watch and making revisions as needed.

In addition to commitment, professionals must also make a realistic appraisal of the impact of the peer program on the center as a whole. In providing more service to greater numbers of students, paraprofessionals increase use of facilities, materials, equipment, and office resources. With the average learning center employing fifteen paraprofessionals at an average rate of five to fifteen hours per week (Burlingame and others, 1982), the student staff can generate between seventy-five and two hundred twenty-five additional hours of client service every week. The resulting increase can easily put a strain on clerical staff who make appointments, keep records, make payrolls, and generally monitor the comings and goings of the paraprofessionals and their clients. All these factors must be considered when determining the critical mass, that is, the optimal number of peers who can provide maximum service without overextending staff and facilities.

Finally, the institution must support the paraprofessional program if it is to succeed. This support should include a philosophical endorsement of the purpose and functions of the peer program, academic credit for training, and financial support for student salaries. Providing academic credit for training gives peers the message that their involvement in the program is an educational experience not just a job. However, since students who complete training are expected to function at a level of competence, commitment, and responsibility that befits a paraprofessional, they must be compensated accordingly.

Management Goals. The overall management of a paraprofessional program has three goals. First, "make it as easy and useful as possible for all program participants by providing a well-controlled structure. Eliminate, as much as possible, chaos, uncertainty, attendance problems, and other unsettling elements which often afflict such programs and undermine student progress" (Solinger, 1978, p. 12). Second, find the proper balance between training and performance. What is the minimal amount and kind of training necessary to produce good performance? What characteristics and skills must the peer possess prior to training, and what can training develop and refine? The best way the director has of answering these questions is to work directly with clients in the capacity in which paraprofessionals will serve. In this way, the director can accurately determine the scope and limits of the peer role and appropriate training objectives. Third, establish good relations and communication with the academic and student affairs units. Since all paraprofessional roles in a learning center involve a blend of student service and academic instruction, it is important for the director to "establish both program and personal credibility with key people in both camps" (Solinger, 1978, p. 12).

These three goals are crucial not only when the program is starting up but throughout the entire course of its history. There is always a need to update and revise policy and procedure, to assess and refine training and duties, and to foster and cement a good relationship with academic and student affairs units on campus.

Recruitment. As Ender points out in Chapter One, both the academic and student affairs units should be involved in recruitment. Invite academic advisors, faculty, student activities directors, and members of the administration to identify and nominate potential candidates. Involving these people during the early phases of the peer program can do much to promote acceptance and support for the program.

Other recruitment sources include current paraprofessionals, student organizations and honorary societies, student development and leadership programs, and student employment and work study. However, in regard to work study, Johnson (1981, p. 90) warns: "While work study funds can be used occasionally, the primary sources for student salaries should be unrestricted, thereby allowing hiring of the most qualified applicants."

Selection. In addition to the characteristics listed earlier in the chapter, the following qualifications play an important part in learning center peer roles: The peer must be a person who is confident, poised, unpretentious, approachable, organized, sensitive to the needs of others, persistent, and patient. The peer must have a genuine enthusiasm for learning, an inquisitive and curious nature, and an above-average and stable grade point average. The emphasis placed on intangible qualities and academic achievement varies with the particular peer role. The tutor must have expertise in course content. The skills counselor must be able to interact with and relate to a wide variety of students with different needs and problems. All paraprofessionals must, however, have ability in both the academic and the interpersonal areas.

The selection interview should accomplish several things: First, all aspects of the peer training and role should be discussed, and candidates should have an opportunity to ask questions. Second, candidates should have an opportunity to present themselves and demonstrate their communication skills. Third, candidates should perform simulation exercises that incorporate the content and processes involved in the peer role. The selection interview should be conducted by professionals and experienced paraprofessionals. Group and individual sessions should both be used so that the candidate's functioning in one-to-one and group interactions can be observed.

Training. Since no interview process is completely foolproof, students should be selected into the program on a provisional basis, and final acceptance should be dependent on successful completion of the training program. Some type of preliminary training should be provided before the trainee is enrolled in the full credit-bearing portion of the program, so that, in the event that the student or the director decides that the student is not suited for the peer role, the student can withdraw without jeopardizing his or her credit load for the term.

The core training program should address three basic areas: the peer role, process skills, and content skills. Topics in the peer role portion of the training include orientation to the learning center, the nature of the peer role and its relationship to the center's functions, procedures and responsibilities, and the nature of the clients whom the center serves. Process skills are needed to carry out the functions of the peer role. Training in process skills should address such topics as the helping interaction, interview and assessment techniques, the conduct of individual and group instructional sessions, communication skills, developmental tasks and crises, basic counseling methods, and referral techniques. Content skills involve the subject matter and knowledge base involved in the peer role. Content skills related to learning center paraprofessional roles include the administration and interpretation of assessment instruments, learning strategies and study skills, behavior and information-processing theory, instructional techniques, and adaptations of learning and instructional methods to modes appropriate for the handicapped and learning-disabled.

Because of time constraints, the core training cannot cover all the issues to the level or depth desired. However, ongoing training sessions can remedy any deficiencies. Ongoing training is also necessary to deal with new issues and concerns, to refresh skills and knowledge, and to prepare for peer specializations.

Supervision and Evaluation of Paraprofessionals. The purpose of supervision is to evaluate the paraprofessional's strengths and weaknesses, to set goals for improving the paraprofessional's performance, and to establish plans for achieving those goals. The frequency, form, and emphasis of supervision is different during the training and posttraining phases.

During the training phase, the purpose of supervision is to evaluate the trainee's progress in achieving proficiency in the content and process skills as demonstrated by the trainee's performance in the experiential components of the training program. The evaluation should emulate the hierarchy and sequence with which topics were presented in the training class. Since the director is unable to observe each individual trainee as often as desired, experienced paraprofessionals can assist with the supervision and evaluation of trainees by serving as co-trainers.

After observing trainees, the co-trainer provides immediate feedback, offers support and encouragement, and discusses any questions or concerns that trainees may have. The co-trainer gives periodic reports to the director. Trainees participate in the evaluation process by submitting weekly reports on their perceptions of what the experiential session accomplished, on the things that went well and the things that could have gone better, and on any personal objectives or goals for upcoming sessions. The director also conducts occasional formal observations of trainees to evaluate individual progress and to assess the progress of the training group as a whole, because the director wants to determine how effective the training has been and what adjustments should be made.

In the posttraining phase, supervision can take the form of a staff meeting, in which paraprofessionals present cases, share new insights and concerns, provide feedback on the program's functioning, work together on new projects, and determine future goals. Here, too, the director conducts a few formal observations and individual supervision sessions with each paraprofessional during the term. However, there should be an open-door policy that allows paraprofessionals timely access to the supervisor. Since the paraprofessional is at the learning center only for a few hours a week, it is very important for him or her to have immediate access to a professional to discuss disturbing situations or to avert a potential crisis with a client.

Evaluation of Paraprofessional Services. Learning centers must keep accurate count of the number of students who use the services and the number of hours of assistance provided. Moreover, clients should be invited to rate and comment on the content, structure, and materials of the program. Client input is a good source of the information needed to determine whether changes or adjustments can be made that will improve the program.

The use of student grade point averages or course grades to evaluate learning programs is questionable, because it is difficult to identify and even more difficult to control all the variables that can affect grades (Boylan, 1981). A better measure of the effectiveness of a learning center program is the client's self-report on behavioral and attitudinal changes that are relevant to the objectives of intervention. For example, the student who reports changes in his or her study skills and how those changes have affected the quality of the student's learning has obviously benefitted from the program. Until those skills are fully embedded and integrated internally, the effects of the change may not be immediately reflected in the student's grades. Thus, even if grades do not reflect change, the program must be judged successful if the student clients feel that the quality of their learning has improved and if they are more confident about and in control of their ability to learn.

Learning Skills Paraprofessionals: Two Examples

The University of Georgia Tutorial Program. The University of Georgia's tutorial program began in the mid 1970s to assist students enrolled in courses of the Developmental Studies Program, which provided remedial education, but in the late 1970s it was made available to any student in core courses.

It is interesting how this came about. As former developmental studies students moved into the general curriculum, they suggested that the tutorial program should be extended to help students make the transition. When tutoring was expanded so that assistance could be provided to former developmental studies students in core courses, regularly admitted students sought help as well. As a result, tutoring was opened to anyone in the core courses. Today, of the 7,000 contacts made each year, 20 percent are with developmental studies students, and 80 percent are with core curriculum students.

The program coordinator places heavy emphasis on paraprofessional self-selection into the program. Potential tutors are made fully aware of the purpose and expectations of the role. They are required to submit a transcript and to have a recommendation checklist completed by two instructors from the subject area in which they intend to tutor. It is made clear to applicants that full acceptance and employment will be offered only if they complete the training course successfully. So, the course is actually an extension of the selection process.

Approximately fifteen tutors are employed each year, but the coordinator has found that eighteen to twenty-five provide maximum service. Each tutor works seven to nine hours per week and generally remains with the program for at least two years. Graduate students and an assistant to the coordinator are responsible for day-to-day supervision, and they are always accessible to the tutors for consultation. The tutors submit brief logs of each session, which include a description of the purpose and content of the session. The logs are the basic means of supervision.

The University of Pittsburgh Math Undergraduate Teaching Assistant Program. The University of Pittsburgh's Learning Skills Center (LSC), a component of the university's Counseling and Student Development Center, serves about 2,000 students annually. It employs about seventy student paraprofessionals in three capacities: study skills counselor, math tutor, and math undergraduate teaching assistant (UTA). This presentation will focus on the UTA program, which emerged from the study skills counselor and math tutor programs. The UTA program is noteworthy because it exemplifies cooperative efforts between a student affairs–based learning center and academic units to make learning skills functions an integral part of a course in math.

In 1978, the mathematics department instituted a new course series designed to help students with a weak background in algebra and trigonometry. The course series gave students the option to take the equivalent of a one-term three-credit algebra and trigonometry course in two two-credit courses. The new courses included two one-hour large-group lectures given by the professor and two one-hour small-group (maximum: twenty students) problem-solving sessions each week. Because of the success of the LSC peer programs in math tutoring and study skills, the mathematics department and the College of Arts and Sciences asked the LSC to select, train, and supervise undergraduates who could serve as teaching assistants for the problem-solving sessions. Within the first year, the new courses and the UTA approach reduced student failure by almost half. The UTA program, which receives financial support from the College of Arts and Sciences and which is operated by the LSC, continues to serve an important function, especially after the institution of a new math requirement in 1982, which primarily involves the two-term algebra and trigonometry courses.

The UTAs work six hours each week. Two hours are spent in conducting the problem-solving sessions, which provide students with an opportunity to reinforce and practice problem-solving approaches to concepts introduced in the lectures and to learn effective methods for studying math. The UTAs also conduct three office hours each week to provide students with individual assistance, and they attend a one-hour supervision session conducted jointly by the mathematics professor and the LSC math specialist who is primarily responsible for the UTAs.

The limits on the UTA's role conform to those presented earlier in this chapter for instructional peer roles. UTAs do not present new instructional material, and they do not grade quizzes or exams. They collect and record homework assignments for the purpose of giving each student individual feedback and comments and for the purpose of monitoring student needs. Homework has little bearing on final grades.

In addition to observation by the LSC math specialist at least twice a term, UTAs are evaluated by students. The results are tabulated, discussed, and reviewed with the individual UTAs. Consistently, UTAs are rated highly by peers on all items, with the highest rating being given to the UTAs' concern for students. In summary, the program is both a success and a benefit for all involved.

References

Boylan, H. R. "Program Evaluation: Issues, Needs, and Realities." In C. C. Walvekar (Ed.), *Assessment of Learning Assistance Services.* New Directions for College Learning Assistance, no. 5. San Francisco: Jossey-Bass, 1981.

Burlingame, G., Daley, P., Kochenour, E., and Oritt, E. "The Role of Paraprofessionals in the Learning Center." Paper presented to the American Personnel and Guidance Association, Detroit, March 1982.

Clowes, D. A. "More Than a Definitional Problem: Remedial, Compensatory, and Developmental Education." *Journal of Developmental and Remedial Education,* 1980, *4* (1), 8–10.

Cross, K. P. *Beyond the Open Door: New Students to Higher Education.* San Francisco: Jossey-Bass, 1971.

Devirian, M. C., Enright, G., and Smith, G. D. "A Survey of Learning Program Centers in U.S. Institutions of Higher Education." In R. Sugimoto (Ed.), *College Learning Skills, Today and Tomorrowland: Proceedings of the Eighth Annual Conference of the Western College Reading Association.* Anaheim, Calif.: Western College Reading Association, 1975.

Enright, G., and Kerstiens, G. "The Learning Center: Toward an Expanded Role." In O. T. Lenning and R. L. Nayman (Eds.), *New Roles for Learning Assistance.* New Directions for College Learning Assistance, no. 2. San Francisco: Jossey-Bass, 1980.

Johnson, D. S. "A Selection and Training Program for Student Paraprofessionals." In F. L. Christ and M. Coda-Messerle (Eds.), *Staff Development for Learning Support Systems.* New Directions for College Learning Assistance, no. 4. San Francisco: Jossey-Bass, 1981.

Maxwell, M. *Improving Student Learning Skills: A Comprehensive Guide to Successful Practices and Programs for Increasing the Performance of Underprepared Students.* San Francisco: Jossey-Bass, 1979.

Sexauer, C., and Koloski, B. "Teachers and Tutors: Toward a Right Relationship." *Journal of Developmental and Remedial Education,* 1981, *4* (3), 26.

Solinger, R. "A Peer Tutoring Program: The Director's Role." *Journal of Developmental and Remedial Education,* 1978, *2* (1), 12, 13, 24.

Georgine Materniak is coordinator of the University of Pittsburgh's Learning Skills Center (LSC) and past chairperson of the American College Personnel Association's Commission on Learning Centers. Since 1974, she has been directly responsible for the creation and implementation of paraprofessional programs at the LSC.

The use of paraprofessionals in academic advising is a significant supplement to existing advising services.

Student Paraprofessionals in Academic Advising

Wesley R. Habley

Many programs described in this sourcebook focus on traditional ways of using students in paraprofessional roles. This chapter describes a relatively new role for paraprofessionals in higher education: academic adviser. It reviews the research on the effectiveness of students as academic advisers, it describes the advantages and disadvantages of using paraprofessionals in academic advising, and it summarizes issues related to the planning and implementation of paraprofessional advising programs. The last section describes four working programs, each of which represents a different level of paraprofessional utilization.

Effectiveness and Satisfaction

A review of the literature on paraprofessional advising programs supports the contention that students perform in academic adviser roles at a level that at least equals, if not exceeds, the level of faculty or professional staff performing the same roles. Three themes emerge from the comparative research on student satisfaction with faculty and paraprofessional academic advisers: First, paraprofessionals score significantly higher than faculty members on interpersonal dimensions of the advising relationship (Murry, 1972; MacAleese, 1974; Habley, 1978). Second, there are no significant differences

S. Ender, R. Winston (Eds.). *Using Students as Paraprofessional Staff.* New
Directions for Student Services, no. 27. San Francisco: Jossey-Bass, September 1984.

between professionals and paraprofessionals on information dimensions of the advising relationship (MacAleese, 1974). Third, there are no significant differences between the students advised by paraprofessionals and the students advised by faculty on such student dimensions as grade point average and probation rate (Brown and Myers, 1975; Zultowski and Catron, 1976). However, attrition rates are significantly lower for students advised by other students (Brown and Myers, 1975). Finally, comparative research on student satisfaction with paraprofessional and professional advisors generally acknowledges that student advisors are as effective as professional advisors and that student advisors are better accepted by clients (Zunker, 1964; Zunker and Brown, 1966; Habley, 1978).

Advantages of Using Paraprofessionals

The use of paraprofessionals has several advantages that are specific to the role of student academic adviser. Habley (1979) cites four advantages that are particularly pertinent to the use of paraprofessionals in academic advising: availability and accessibility, staffing flexibility, systematic input on program effectiveness, and increased organizational dynamics.

Availability and Accessibility. Student advisers are available to assist other students in locations and at times when other advising personnel are generally not available. This is particularly useful for an advising program that functions during daytime working hours. Whether there is a structured office role for paraprofessionals, whether they are required to live in university housing, or both, paraprofessional advisers are available and accessible to other students in informal settings by virtue of their membership in the student peer group.

Staffing Flexibility. The paraprofessional program provides staffing flexibility during peak advising periods. This advantage is significant during registration, when the advising system must deal with large numbers of students and when quality advising becomes nearly impossible. As part-time advisers whose work loads can be increased during peak periods, paraprofessional advisers provide additional human resources at a time when the advising program most needs them.

Systematic Input on Program Effectiveness. Student advisers recognize problems and challenge inadequacies in the advising system because they are more attuned than professionals to the effect that advising has on their peers. As a result of peer group membership, student advisers are exposed to advising concerns that are usually not brought to the attention of faculty or professional advising staff. The channeling of these concerns can lead to improvements in the advising system.

Increased Organizational Dynamics. Generally, those who are charged with advising responsibilities do so on a recurring basis. Such a pattern can lead to a closed organizational system which operates on shared understandings and precedents. Such a maintenance pattern will almost inevitably be challenged by student advisers. As a result of their identification with peers and their enthusiasm for the role, they provide other advising staff with a stimulus to change and improve, and they can make the system more dynamic and more open so that services can be delivered more effectively. Recommendations made by student advisers include the development of an intake system to ensure that students whose questions require short answers can receive assistance without having to schedule an appointment or wait for an adviser to fit them in between scheduled appointments; the development of media presentations on topics—registration, the general education program, and degree plan completion—that affect all students; and the development of satellite advising stations in residence halls, student union, and classroom buildings.

Disadvantages of Using Paraprofessionals

The use of students in academic advising also has some significant disadvantages, which have been cited in the literature (Zultowski and Catron, 1976; Habley, 1978; Goldberg, 1981). These disadvantages are discussed here not to discourage the implementation of a paraprofessional advising program but to encourage program planners to address potential problems in the planning stage, so that the paraprofessional advising program will become even more effective when it is implemented.

Faculty Sensitivity. One disadvantage of using paraprofessionals that can become more acute in an advising program relates to the role of faculty. On most campuses, faculty are the academic advisers. Because advising continues to be a faculty prerogative, faculty may either be skeptical of or feel threatened by a paraprofessional academic advising program. This phenomenon is natural in any organization that contemplates a change in responsibilities. The extent to which faculty can be incorporated into the paraprofessional advising program will to a great degree mediate the faculty's concern. In fact, it is necessary to involve faculty in the program if it is to succeed. One way in which faculty support can be gained is by sharing research on the effectiveness of paraprofessional advising programs. Other suggestions for promoting faculty involvement are presented in later sections of this chapter.

Supervision. The success of a paraprofessional advising program also rests on the quality of the interaction between the paraprofessionals and their immediate supervisors. Although this factor is a concern for all paraprofessional programs, it is particularly acute in an advising program, where accurate information is imperative. As a result of this information dimension, paraprofessional activity requires constant review. Traditional advising programs may not be staffed by individuals who have the ability or the desire to train and supervise student advisers. The absence of such individuals makes it impossible to implement a peer advising program.

Subjectivity. One of the more pervasive concerns raised by paraprofessional advising programs involves the perceived lack of objectivity that results from the paraprofessional's dual status as student and adviser. The temptation of advising students away from difficult courses and instructors is present, and it can constitute a major criticism of the "student advising program."

Specialization. Because of the enormous amount of curricular and procedural information required to function effectively as an adviser, paraprofessionals must specialize in a single major or in a group of related majors. This specialization is not a disadvantage per se, but it can present problems if the student adviser is called on to advise a student who is either undecided about a major or who is considering changing majors. As a result, student advisers should only advise students who are relatively committed to a major related to the student adviser's background. Although student advisers can support the advising of undecided students, such activity should not be their primary advising responsibility.

Accountability. Four factors contribute to concern for accountability of paraprofessional advisors: The specificity of information required for the role, the possible consequences of sharing incorrect information with a student, the short time for which an individual paraprofessional serves, and increasing litigation of issues related to academic advising. In reality, however, the issue of accountability is no different here than it is in any supervisor-employee relationship. The supervisor is ultimately responsible for the work of his or her subordinates. Thus, the supervisor of paraprofessional advisers must make sure that they receive thorough training, that evaluation and other feedback mechanisms are working, and that the information being shared is both accurate and appropriate to the student who is being advised. To secure accountability of this form, the supervisor should require complete conference notes for each contact. The supervisor should review all conference notes and direct the paraprofessional to follow up individually with an advisee when an error has been made, a misunderstanding has arisen, or inappropriate advice has been given.

Program Planning Issues

Program planning issues include defining the population to be served, assessing faculty readiness, and identifying ethical issues in the program. It is important to note here that advising programs must be designed for the institutional context, and it is unlikely that any model for the use of paraprofessional advisers can be transferred from one institution to another intact. As Barman and Benson (1981, p. 33) point out, "academic advising programs in higher education are as diversified as the missions and purposes of the colleges and universities in the United States. It is important that they be designed and implemented to meet the unique needs of each student body."

Defining the Population to be Served. While it is probably true that a paraprofessional advising program can provide significant benefits to all types of students, it is absolutely necessary for those planning the program to identify the students whom paraprofessional advisers will serve. Five factors should be considered when defining the population to be served: the level of the advisee's commitment to a major; the advisee's class standing, the advisee's academic ability, the advisee's academic standing, and the extent to which the advisee can be considered to have special needs. Each student presents unique advising needs that dictate differential approaches to the selection, training, and responsibilities of paraprofessional academic advisers. It is obvious that no paraprofessional adviser can be expected to meet all the advising needs of all members of the student body. As a result, it is critical to develop a clear definition of the population to be served by student advisers.

Assessing Faculty Readiness. There is probably no greater deterrent to the development of a paraprofessional advising program than resistance from a faculty that is skeptical of or that feels threatened by the perceived usurpation of authority that such a program may represent. If faculty cannot be convinced of the value of paraprofessional advising, the program will encounter great difficulty. However, there are cogent rejoinders with which faculty opposition to paraprofessional advising can be met. First, faculty can be shown that paraprofessional advisers will release some of their time, which they can devote to scholarly activity, research, and instructional development. Second, most faculty are interested in advising students who are committed to the discipline; change-of-major statistics will persuade them that many of the students whom they advise will in all probability change their majors. Third, faculty who receive assurances that they will play a major role in the recruitment, selection, and training of paraprofessional advisers become more willing to support such a program. Finally, faculty who can be convinced that the paraprofessional program will enhance, rather than replace, the faculty advising system will be ready to accept and support the concept.

Identifying Ethical Issues. As in all paraprofessional programs in higher education, the success of a paraprofessional advising program must be measured in terms of the growth and development of the students whom it serves. If the peer relationship is structured effectively, it is a powerful mechanism for assisting students' development.

At least two ethical issues require attention in the planning phase. The first ethical issue deals with the imposition of values by the paraprofessional adviser. The temptation to advise students away from difficult courses or instructors is always present, and it can lead to the demise of the program. If the program merely formalizes the student grapevine on courses and instructors, then it undermines the concept of student development. In fact, institutionalization of the informal student information network, which can be woefully inaccurate, can prove harmful both to the institution and to students. Therefore, the philosophical underpinnings of a paraprofessional advising program should stress the value of accurate information that is objectively shared with students, and it should stress that value judgments regarding the teaching-and-learning process must be withheld. The training of paraprofessionals should be firmly planted in the notions that value judgments are subjective, that these judgments are the prerogative only of advisees, and that student decision making based on accurate information is the desired outcome of quality academic advising.

The second ethical issue involves confidentiality. Since few undergraduates have been called on to deal with this issue, planners of paraprofessional programs must clearly define the conditions under which confidential materials will be shared with student advisers. Besides appreciating the confidentiality of student records, the paraprofessional adviser must realize that the advising interaction itself is an ethically confidential interaction. The misuse or abuse of confidential information shared in the presumed privacy of the advising contact will diminish students' confidence in the program and eventually cause its downfall. As a result of increasing concern for the confidentiality of student records, many institutions have developed detailed policies on access to such records. Some institutions prohibit student employees from access to student records. Because effective paraprofessional advising cannot take place in the absence of student records, such policies have to be modified, or they virtually dictate the scope of a paraprofessional academic advising program.

Program Implementation Issues

From the broad planning issues raised by a paraprofessional advising program we may pass to several facets of program implementation. Although program implementation issues have been addressed in a general way in Chapter One, we can consider those issues here as they relate to the development of a paraprofessional advising program. It bears repeating that there is no single formula for the development and administration of a paraprofessional advising program. Rather, a successful program is measured by its ability to meet the developmental needs of student clients while supporting the mission and purpose of the institution.

Selection Criteria. It is important to delineate the selection criteria for paraprofessional advisers clearly, and these criteria should be communicated in the application process. However, it is just as important that the selection criteria should not be so specific as to limit the development of a quality candidate pool from which final selections can be made. Two selection criteria are pertinent to a paraprofessional advising program: class standing and academic performance.

First, the selection criteria should specify the class standing necessary for selection as a paraprofessional adviser. Freshmen cannot be candidates, because they lack the experience needed to function effectively in the role. At the same time, it is a mistake to restrict the program to seniors, because such a criterion means that an entire paraprofessional staff must be selected and trained every year. Thus, it is desirable for the program to require freshman or sophomore standing at the time of application and sophomore, junior, or senior status at the time of employment.

Second, the selection criteria should consider academic performance. Although several options are available, only two are viable. The first option requires a record of academic excellence as a prerequisite to service as a student adviser. This approach may be less successful than one would anticipate. High-achievers do not always make the best paraprofessional advisers, because they have encountered few academic problems, because they may not understand the full range of those problems, or because they do not empathize with students who are having difficulty negotiating the academic bureaucracy. In addition, high-achieving students sometimes have difficulty balancing the demands of the adviser and student roles.

The criterion for academic performance should exceed the minimum performance required for academic good standing at the institution but not to the extent that only the most academically capable students can become student advisers. There are several advantages to this suggestion. First, setting academic performance qualifications above the institution's minimum standards for good standing is a strong selling point to faculty. Second, because the role can require a substantial commitment of time, it is best not to employ individuals whose academic standing could be jeopardized by an extensive time commitment to advising. Third, typical students may have a broad understanding of policies and procedures gained through personal experience. Last, for a paraprofessional program to be successful, advisers must be representative of the entire student body.

Compensation. The second issue that must be considered in the implementation of a peer advising program is compensation. A wide variety of options are available. The first, and probably the most desirable, is to make the position a salaried one. Some paraprofessional advising programs pay student advisers an hourly wage, while others provide a fixed stipend for the role with regular payments distributed over the period of employment. While compensation at an hourly rate makes a great deal of flexibility in staffing possible and provides the supervisor with an immediate control mechanism, a fixed salary or stipend has three significant advantages. First, it allows for the setting of equal expectations for all student advisers. Second, it allows the supervisor to take advantage of staffing flexibility during peak periods without increasing personnel costs. Of course, student advisers must have a clear understanding that the time commitment to the role varies with the need for services. Third, it may assure an element of professionalism greater than that which hourly employment can obtain.

Another way of compensating student advisers is through waiver of tuition or room and board. Although this option is popular, it poses three significant problems. First, it may be difficult to stimulate paraprofessionals to improve their performance once payment has been made. Second, if it becomes necessary to terminate the employment relationship, the fiscal implications become difficult to manage. Third, if operating dollars are used, the tuition and room and board increases require the supervisor to justify increasing the allocation for the program. If operating funds remain stable while college costs increase, the outcome is a loss of paraprofessional positions. As a result, this method of compensation should be scrutinized carefully before it is adopted.

Still another way of compensating paraprofessional academic advisers is by offering elective course credit. The institution's curricular approval process determines how useful this compensation mechanism will be. Two other problems are inherent in this approach. First, students in highly sequential programs may not have room in their programs for electives, and as a result they may screen themselves out of the program. Second, compensaton for second-year advisers poses a special problem. If the course provides the learning experiences necessary to function effectively in the role of student adviser, then there is little reward for students who reenroll, and other compensation must be provided.

One other method for compensating paraprofessional advisers is not extrinsic at all. If other methods of compensation are not viable, volunteerism should not be overlooked. Although a volunteer program gives supervisors less control, it offers the intrinsic motivation of providing assistance to other students. A volunteer program can be organized with the aid of honor societies, department clubs, or student government. While the many problems associated with administration of a volunteer paraprofessional advising program are not delineated here, such an approach is worthy of exploration if other forms of remuneration are not available.

Recruitment and Selection Process. The third implementation issue concerns the development of a recruitment and selection strategy that secures the best paraprofessional advisers available. The recruitment process for these positions is similar to other paraprofessional roles. Here, however, faculty must play an integral part. First, faculty identify candidates for the position. Each faculty member should be given a general description of the role and a list of the qualifications needed. Not only does this procedure ensure wider dissemination of recruitment materials, but involvement of faculty in recruitment improves faculty understanding of the student adviser's role.

Faculty involvement is also essential in the selection process. At a minimum, each candidate should have a recommendation from at least one faculty member. Participation by faculty in the interview process should also be encouraged. Both activities serve to increase the efficacy of the paraprofessional program in the minds of faculty.

Supervision. Supervision is another important administrative aspect of paraprofessional advising programs. The provision of adequate staff time to accomplish training, supervision, and evaluation is a true hidden cost factor of such programs. Depending on the scope of training, the span of supervision, and the ongoing support for the paraprofessional program, substantial resources must be directed away from service delivery and devoted to the development and maintenance of the program. Professional or faculty advisers may not have the ability or the desire to become trainers and supervisors of student advisers.

However, the success of a paraprofessional program hinges more on the quality of the relationship between the paraprofessionals and their immediate supervisor than on any other. Therefore, it is extremely important for those in supervisory roles to have both the ability and the desire to work with students. Even more important, those who supervise must be given ample time to conduct a comprehensive training program and perform ongoing supervisory functions.

Training. Because one of the major peaks of activity for academic advisers occurs at the beginning of the term, preservice training for new paraprofessionals must be carefully designed. Although extensive preservice training is desirable, many factors make it virtually impossible to provide paraprofessionals with all the skills and information that they need in order to function at maximum efficiency on their first day in the role. As a result, preservice training adopts the survival approach. Even in programs that allocate four or five days for intense preservice training, only the most basic information can be presented effectively. At a minimum, preservice training should focus on registration procedures, major requirements, minor requirements, general education, and basic academic policies and procedures. There is simply too little time to cover other advising issues in depth.

Following the preservice training program and registration activities, a full scale in-service training program should be implemented. The in-service program should have several foci. As in other paraprofessional programs, the in-service training for student advisers should emphasize peer counseling skills. Training in this area includes attending behavior, open-ended responses, paraphrasing, reflection, summarizinag, goal setting, decision making, action planning, and nonverbal behavior.

The second focus of the in-service program should be on extending the information base whose foundations were laid in the preservice training program. Although there may be an unwritten expectation that paraprofessionals will master the information completely, it is useful to focus on the information sources from which the information that may be needed can be gleaned. Review should stress that paraprofessionals should know where to find answers, not that they should have those answers on immediate recall.

The third focus of in-service paraprofessional training is on advising procedures. This area includes such things as scheduling student contacts, handling advising files, making referrals, consulting with other advisers, preparing conference notes, and a variety of other activities that are operational in nature.

Finally, motivated paraprofessional advisers who have been trained in helping skills may have difficulty balancing the paraprofessional role with the more important role of being a student. To counteract this difficulty, in-service training should address time management, interview termination, and referral techniques. If these issues are addressed, the pervasive problem of paraprofessional burnout can be minimized.

Evaluation. Evaluation is another essential component of a paraprofessional advising program. It is critical for the work of student advisers to be supervised closely and for feedback on performance to be both immediate and ongoing. To accomplish this end, a record-keeping system should be established to document advisee contact with paraprofessionals through conference notes. Not only must the written record be a strong facet of the program, but the supervisor should also review all conference notes in order to provide feedback to paraprofessional advisers. Directing an adviser to contact an advisee and correct an advising error or misconception minimizes the problems that may surface later in the advisee's academic career, and it provides an essential accountability mechanism.

Advisees should be asked to provide feedback on the performance of paraprofessional advisers. Information gained from advisees gives the student adviser recognition, and it points to possible areas for improvement. Both recognition and improvement are essential to the well-being of the program. The feedback instrument should be administered after every advising interaction, and it should be concise. At a minimum, three factors should be assessed: availability, knowledge, and concern for the student's welfare.

Finally, self-evaluation can be a useful tool for paraprofessional advisers. If the program employs skilled paraprofessionals, they should have some meaningful insights into their own performance. Self-evaluation should review strengths and weaknesses, areas of responsibility that are unclear, and goal setting. In some ways, self-evaluation can be the most productive evaluative technique, because it can take place in a nonthreatening environment, and because it is focused on the adviser's continuing development.

Existing Models of Paraprofessional Utilization

The University of Montana. The University of Montana provides an excellent example of a paraprofessional advising program. In its program, thirty student advisers provide one-on-one service to students. Each paraprofessional is assigned to a small number of undecided students. For these students, the student advisers have the same advising authority as faculty members who advise declared majors. In addition, the student advisers are required to serve in the Office of Advising and Retention, where, in addition to meeting with their assigned undecided students, they serve as resource persons for any student who has general questions relating to the academic advising process. Paraprofessional advisers also work on a variety of special projects, such as contacting nondegree students who are reaching the maximum number of credits that can be transferred into a degree program. Finally, the student advisers participate in delivery of the study skills program and the early warning identification system.

One unique element of the University of Montana's paraprofessional advising program is the combination of compensation and training in a course credit component. Students who opt to participate in the program receive one quarter-hour of credit for independent study in the School of Education for each thirty hours of service to the program. Grades are contracted for at the beginning of the year, and each student adviser earns three or four quarter-hours of credit for a year's service. In addition to participating in fourteen hours of preservice training, the independent study course meets at least once a month for a two-hour block of time.

University of Wisconsin–Eau Claire. The University of Wisconsin–Eau Clair, a public liberal arts university, uses paraprofessionals at two levels. At the first level, students act as assistants to faculty and professional advisers during the summer orientation program. Each paraprofessional is paired with an orientation adviser and assigned advisees in a major or group of majors that is related to the background of the adviser and the paraprofessional. The paraprofessional adviser is responsible not only for the traditional activities performed by orientation assistants but also for the planning and delivery of a media-supported program on academic policies and procedures, general education, and other topics of academic import. The orientation adviser and the paraprofessional share this program. Paraprofessionals are also responsible for preliminary course selection, which takes place on the first day of a two-day orientation session. At that session, the paraprofessional works with individual students to develop a list of courses and alternative selections that is discussed and verified by the orientation adviser at an appointment on the following day.

During the academic year, a select group of orientation paraprofessionals works in the office of academic and career advising. Because the office's primary service is to undeclared students, the role of paraprofessionals in that office is limited to program support. Paraprofessionals acting in this role have developed a media-supported program called "The Registration Game," which is delivered in university residence halls as well as in the University Center. Paraprofessionals also staff a "help table" in the University Arena during registration. Finally, they make telephone contacts with students advised in the office of academic and career advising. Each term, paraprofessionals contact new undeclared students, students in academic difficulty, or others identified by the professional staff. This outreach activity helped to increase student contact fourfold during the first year in which it was implemented.

Marymount Manhattan College. The paraprofessional advising program at Marymount Manhattan College is volunteer. Forty-five student advisers serve an average of two to four hours per week. Since all students are assigned to faculty advisers, paraprofessionals do not have authority to sign class schedules or approve program changes. Rather, paraprofessionals provide a variety of support services to the student body. For example, they staff a peer adviser booth in a high-visibility location, serve as co-facilitators of the freshman seminar program, and make referrals to campus support services. No student adviser spends time in an academic advising office as a matter of course, but student advisers are responsible for being available in department offices to serve students who have the same major.

University of Wisconsin–Whitewater. The University of Wisconsin–Whitewater, a comprehensive undergraduate public university, is experiencing major enrollments in business and business-related programs. Whitewater's advising program is fairly traditional, in that all students are advised by faculty members in the department in which they major. However, because of the increasing demand for advising services, the campus developed an academic advising office, which is administered by the executive director of student administrative services and which is staffed by a graduate assistant and nine undergraduate paraprofessional advisers. Six serve the traditional student population, and three serve nontraditional students. The primary role of these paraprofessional advisers is to be an advising resource to all students on campus. In that capacity, paraprofessionals meet with students in all majors and at all levels of class standing to provide general advice on policies, procedures, and general course selection. They have no authority to sign documents that require adviser approval. That authority is held only by the student's assigned faculty adviser. Paraprofessionals also serve as referral agents to other campus programs and services.

References

Barman, C. R., and Benson, P. A. "Peer Advising: A Working Model." *NACADA Journal,* 1981, *1* (1), 33–40.

Brown, C. R., and Myers, R. "Student Versus Faculty Curriculum Advising." *Journal of College Student Personnel,* 1975, *16* (8), 226–231.

Goldberg, L. "Peer Advising: A Supplement to, but Not a Substitute for Faculty Advising." *NACADA Journal,* 1981, *1* (1), 41–43.

Habley, W. R. "Adviser Satisfaction with Student, Faculty, and Advisement Center Academic Advisors." Unpublished doctoral dissertation, Illinois State University, 1978.

Habley, W. R. "The Advantages and Disadvantages of Using Students as Academic Advisors." *NASPA Journal,* 1979, *17* (1), 46–51.

MacAleese, R. "A Comparative Evaluation of Faculty and Student Paraprofessional Academic Advisement Programs." Unpublished doctoral dissertation, Florida State University, 1974.

Murry, J. P. "The Comparative Effectiveness of Student-to-Student and Faculty Advising Programs." *Journal of College Student Personnel,* 1972, *13* (6), 562–566.

Zultowski, W. H., and Catron, D. W. "Students as Curriculum Advisors: Revisited." *Journal of College Student Personnel,* 1976, *17* (3), 199–204.

Zunker, V. G. "A Comparison of the Effectiveness of Student and Certified Counselors in a Selected Program of Academic Adjustment Guidance." Unpublished doctoral dissertation, University of Houston, 1964.

Zunker, V. G., and Brown, W. F. "Comparative Effectiveness of Student and Professional Counselors." *Personnel and Guidance Journal,* 1966, *44* (8), 738–743.

Wesley R. Habley is director of academic and career advising at the University of Wisconsin–Eau Claire. Besides serving as a consultant in academic and career advising, he has published on organizational structures in academic advising, and he has been active in the development of the National Academic Advising Association, which he served first as a member of the board of directors for the East Central Region, then as treasurer.

Due in part to the frequency and intimacy of their contact with residents, resident assistants have great potential to influence students' lives positively.

Student Paraprofessionals in Residence Halls

Roger B. Winston, Jr.
Marcy S. Ullom
Charles J. Werring

The college residence hall was probably the first student affairs agency to use students as paraprofessionals in systematic and sustained programs. Without question, housing programs use more students in paraprofessional roles than any other campus agency today. Students were first used in residence halls to maintain order and to serve as liaison between administration and students. Their roles have evolved, and on many campuses today they are peer helpers and environmental managers. There is still a great deal of diversity in the expectations of these paraprofessionals.

This chapter presents a philosophy of residence hall programs that is based on student development concepts. With this philosophy as a foundation, we specify the roles and responsibilities of resident assistants; we identify the ethical and legal issues; we discuss recruitment, selection, training, supervision, and evaluation of paraprofessional staff; and we outline some approaches to program evaluation. Finally, we describe two residence hall programs that make innovative use of paraprofessionals.

S. Ender, R. Winston (Eds.). *Using Students as Paraprofessional Staff.* New Directions for Student Services, no. 27. San Francisco: Jossey-Bass, September 1984.

Residence Hall Philosophy

Because of the behavior problems experienced when groups of students, especially young men, lived in close proximity, residence halls were often viewed as a necessary evil. Consequently, their primary function was to provide custodial care. Staff went about their work with students in loco parentis and sought to provide services that supported or complemented the development of the mind and that maintained acceptable social conduct. Of upmost importance was meeting students' needs for a relatively low-cost place to sleep, shower, store belongings, and sometimes study.

In the early 1970s, concepts associated with the movement that has become known as student development began to emerge. The basic principles of student development (Blimling and Miltenberger, 1981; Brown, 1980; DeCoster and Mable, 1980; Miller and Prince, 1976) apply to student housing. The basic purpose of higher education is the education of the whole person, not just his or her intellect. Educators can be more effective in educating the whole person by understanding the psychosocial and intellectual developmental sequences and processes that students experience and by creating opportunities consistent with those processes that challenge students to realize their full potential. The total environment in which a student lives—not just classroom, library, and laboratory—directly affects his or her education and learning. Students are capable of making decisions about their own best interests. They need instruction about decison-making processes; they need information about the developmental issues that students face, and they need data about themselves in such areas as careers, interpersonal relationships, and changing relationships with parents; they need opportunities to examine their values and ethical system and occasions on which to practice new skills and behavior and receive feedback; and they need support and encouragement to take risks. Finally, residence hall staff can best help students to realize their potential by assessing their needs and wants and by creating structures and environments that allow them to meet their needs.

Riker and DeCoster (1971) developed a scheme based on Maslow's hierarchy of needs that graphically displays the basic purposes of a housing program within the framework of student development. This scheme consists of five levels. Levels one and two are concerned with physical facilities; level three concerns administrative structures, policies, rules, and their enforcement; while levels four and five are concerned with interpersonal environments that challenge and support students as they become better educated, more productive, and more competent persons, workers, and citizens. The basic physical needs must be met before students can even encounter educational and intellectual development issues. Therefore, housing programs must assure that there is a safe, esthetically unobjectionable, and nonthreatening physical facility—basic management functions—before the educational mission can be addressed.

Roles and Responsibilities of Resident Assistants

The roles and responsibilities that student paraprofessionals assume in housing are related directly to the goals of the program in which they are employed. This is often reflected in the titles given to holders of the paraprofessional position. During the 1950s and earlier, they were often called *proctors,* which accurately reflected their principal role as enforcers of rules. In the 1960s, they generally came to be known as *resident assistants* or *resident advisors,* which reflected the change in the responsibilities assigned to them—moving away from being primarily a disciplinarian toward a role that included active efforts to be a peer helper.

In addition to providing adequate physical facilities, housing programs that have the education of students as their goal often use student paraprofessionals, who are called *resident assistants* (RAs). Resident assistants fulfill seven roles: model of effective student, peer helper, information and referral agent, socializer, leader and organizer, clerical worker, and limit setter and conflict mediator.

Model of Effective Student. The RA is an institutionally designated role model. Residents watch the RA's behavior carefully, both when he or she is performing official duties and when he or she is simply studying and interacting socially. When the college hires the RA, it says that the student is an effective student who is worthy of emulation. How RAs manage their personal lives, perform academically, and approach the college experience teach those with whom they live by example.

Peer Helper. Substantial research has documented that paraprofessionals trained in the use of peer helping and interpersonal communications skills can be effective, often as effective as trained professionals (Newton, 1974; Scroggins and Ivey, 1978; Zunker and Brown, 1966). In the peer helper role, RAs must establish relationships of mutual trust and respect, communicate their willingness to be of assistance, and make a commitment to expend the time and energy required to help residents deal with their personal concerns. However, RAs should not be expected to be psychotherapists. Generally, they can deal effectively with students as students encounter typical developmental issues or tasks primarily by listening, showing warmth and support, providing information, and helping students to analyze problem situations and formulate plans. Students who require a greater depth of intervention should be referred to professional counselors. RAs should be trained to identify residents with acute problems and inform college officials so that residents can get the professional assistance that they need.

Information and Referral Agent. Resident assistants are expected to be knowledgeable about the college's services, personnel, programs, policies, procedures, and rules. Accurate information is prized on a college campus. RAs can affect student use of the services that an institution provides by spreading the word that a certain office is helpful and by directing residents to appropriate places and eliminating the runaround. Also, RAs can encourage residents to seek assistance for problems or concerns that lie beyond their own level of competence. Students often need support and encouragement to take the risk to confront their problems; RAs can be effective in providing that support.

Socializer. One important role that RAs traditionally have is to get to know fellow residents and help them to form a cohesive group and develop a sense of community. There are three levels in this process: acquaintance (learning names, background information, and personality characteristics); establishment of an accepting atmosphere in which residents can form friendships and articulate personal values and aspirations; and creation of an interpersonal climate characterized by trust, supportiveness, openness, and confidence that encourages students to gain the maximum from the higher education experience (Mable and DeCoster, 1980).

Leader and Organizer. RAs are in de facto leadership positions. Basic leadership and organizational skills are required to help residents come together and form a group that has a collective identity. Some housing programs expect RAs to use their leadership skills to establish and coordinate social and educational programs in the hall units. Other programs ask RAs to use their leadership skills primarily in developing a sense of community, but they hold it more appropriate for non–RAs to initiate and assume responsibility for unit programming. RAs need group leadership skills.

Clerical Worker. Most housing programs expect RAs to collect information from residents, to inventory and inspect rooms and furnishings, to report maintenance and housekeeping needs, and to communicate information and policies to residents. This clerical role, while not as glamorous as some other roles, must be filled effectively if residence halls are to accomplish their educational mission.

Limit Setter and Conflict Mediator. The parental rules of the 1960s and earlier have been replaced by more legalistic regulations relating to five areas: the health, safety, and well-being of the college community; landlord-lessee relationships; state, local, and federal laws; regulations necessary for the smooth functioning of high-density living units; and regulations related to the academic mission of the institution (Blimling and Miltenberger, 1981). RAs play a critical educational function in helping residents to learn the rules for community living and to understand why the rules were established. RAs are also expected to intervene in personal conflicts, often between roommates, and help to find solutions. These are the roles that generally cause RAs the most anxiety and that often conflict with their expectations about being a peer helper. That is, RAs are expected to be "cop-counselors" (Upcraft and Pilato, 1982). This inherent conflict is built into the position, and it can never be completely eliminated. RAs who are able to communicate primarily through their actions that the rules have a purpose, that the violator of a rule chooses the consequences, and that the RA has no personal antagonism for and receives no satisfaction from reprimanding a resident are best able to handle the roles of both helper and disciplinarian.

Legal and Ethical Issues

Several legal and ethical issues are particularly pertinent to RAs and their supervisors. The legal issues that should be discussed with RAs and for which housing policies for staff guidance need to be formulated include search of rooms, tort liability, and privacy rights.

The Fourth Amendment to the U.S. Constitution provides protection against unreasonable search and seizure by government officials. There is no legal precedent about whether housing officials at public colleges may enter student rooms without permission. Courts have ruled that evidence obtained in a warrantless search at a public college cannot be introduced as evidence in a criminal trial. Rooms may be entered for necessary maintenance, inventory, and health and safety inspections without permission. Private colleges can govern searches through the housing contract, since the Fourth Amendment does not apply there (Pavela, 1983). This area is legally complicated. Housing administrators, in consultation with legal counsel, should formulate precise rules about entering students' rooms without permission, and they should train RAs in applying these rules.

Tort liability is another legal area in which RAs need training. "A tort is a civil wrong consisting of an act or omission (other than a breach of contract) for which the courts will provide a remedy in the form of an action for damages" (Moore and Murray, 1983, p. 67). RAs need to be aware of torts related to negligence. For example, if a RA fails to report needed repairs promptly and a resident is injured as a result, the resident may have grounds for a successful suit against the RA, housing officials, and the college.

The privacy rights of residents are another area in which RAs need guidance. The regulations adopted to implement the Family Educational Rights and Privacy Act of 1974 lay out specific rules about what constitutes a record, who has access to records and what information may be made public. Housing administrators need to educate RAs about the compiling of information about residents and about maintaining its security.

Two areas of professional ethics are of particular interest to RAs and their supervisors: romantic relationships and confidentiality. For both paraprofessional and professional staff who live in residence halls, there is a fine line between work and personal life. Because of the closeness in ages, the esprit de corps in a good staff group, and the constant social interaction between RAs and their supervisors, romantic relationships sometimes develop. When this happens, the effectiveness of all concerned, including the other RAs, is affected. Consequently, the American College Personnel Association's ethical and professional standards state that "sexual relationships with staff members or students for whom one has supervisory or evaluative responsibilities have high potential for causing personal damage and for limiting the exercise of professional responsibilities and are therefore unprofessional and unethical" (American College Personnel Association, 1981, p. 185).

Knowing when to keep information confidential sometimes causes ethical dilemmas for RAs. As a general rule, information learned in counseling-type relationships should be kept confidential. However, the distinction between counseling and other types of relationships is often unclear for RAs. For example, Steve comes to the RA to discuss problems in his relationship with his parents—a counseling-type issue. During the session, Steve tells the RA that part of his problem with his parents stems from his use of illegal drugs, which he keeps in his room. What are the RA's responsibilities if the residence hall has a rule against possession of prohibited drugs? The American College Personnel Association ethical and professional standards require that students should be informed of "the nature and/or limits of confidentiality in noncounseling as well as [in] counseling relations" (American College Personnel Association, 1981, p. 184). Also, RAs who learn of conditions that are likely to cause harm to a resident or to others have the responsibility to inform the authorities in order to prevent harm (American College Personnel Association, 1981). RAs need to discuss these issues and formulate plans to inform residents about these limits without erecting barriers that inhibit the formation of helping relationships.

Recruitment and Selection

Three basic issues underlie the RA selection process: who, what, and how (Upcraft and Pilato, 1982). The first issue refers to professional staff and administrators, current RAs, and residents. Each of these groups has a unique perspective and a unique relationship to potential staff members; each group can offer insight and expertise to the process, and each group should propose candidates.

The recruitment and selection of residence hall paraprofessionals has been called complicated, redundant, and costly, and it is often time-consuming (Tibbits, 1977). One study found that selection by peer ratings alone is as effective as selection by more conventional methods. According to Tibbits, professional staff members and students have similar expectations of residence hall paraprofessionals.

Current residence hall paraprofessionals know the job and have an excellent perspective from which to judge. Students' input is important, because they must live with the results. However, RAs generally lack the experience and theoretical background of professionals, and they are likely to select RAs who are most like themselves, the only models they have seen. This builds a closed, self-perpetuating system. Professional staff views and understanding of campus and departmental needs surpass the viewpoint of RAs. Professional staff most intimately involved in the day-to-day workings of training and supervising should make the final selection decision after input from students and experienced RAs.

The second issue includes the establishment of criteria and the identification of selection techniques. Selection criteria, weighed by the goals of the housing program, include demonstrated academic achievement; a warm, friendly personality; good basic interpersonal skills; emotional stability; ability to cope with stress and ambiguity; and ability to accept people with different values or backgrounds (Cannon and Peterman, 1973; Delworth and others, 1974; Greenleaf, 1974; Upcraft and Pilato, 1982). Selection criteria should be directly linked with the position requirements.

The selection process should obtain sufficient information about a candidate to allow that individual's potential for the position to be assessed. The third issue answers how that information can be obtained. The individual interview, leaderless discussion groups, role playing, standardized instruments, and participation in training seminars are some of the methods that have been suggested (Bumba and others, 1980; German, 1979; Greenleaf, 1974; Upcraft and Pilato, 1982).

Interviews are the traditional way of getting to know candidates. Both interviewers and interviewees are allowed flexibility in directing the discussion. However, as a selection tool, interviews are only as good as the interviewer's skills and the objectivity of selection criteria. Leaderless discussion groups and role playing enable the selection committee to observe candidates' skills and ability to assess, confront, and bring a simulated situation to closure. While this technique offers a firsthand view of the candidates, observers should recognize that candidates may not be familiar with the implementation of organizational philosophy, specific rules and regulations, or the characteristics and features of a particular unit, staff, or supervisor. Since the situation is somewhat contrived, some students become overly nervous and do not give an accurate picture of their skills.

Standardized instruments have also been used as part of the selection process. The Personal Orientation Inventory (Atkinson and others, 1973; Kipp, 1979; Schroeder and Wills, 1973), the California Psychological Inventory (Hall and Creed, 1979; Morton, 1975–76; Murphy and Ortenzi, 1966), the Edwards Personal Preference Schedule (German, 1979; Murphy and Ortenzi, 1966), the Personality Research Form (Klockars and Walkup, 1980), and the Strong Vocational Interest Blank (Murphy and Ortenzi, 1966) are some of the instruments that have been used. However, none has accounted for sufficient variance to warrant use as a primary selection tool. Thus, candidates must often commit to participation in training before being appointed to the position. Professional staff then have an opportunity to observe candidates' skills and actions for a longer period of time.

Training

Most residence hall RAs come to the position with raw skills and with the potential to develop these skills. It is the responsibility of professional staff to assess resident and RA needs and then to develop and implement an appropriate training program. After selection, training is the next most critical component in the development of a successful residence hall paraprofessional program. A comprehensive training program should be developed with the philosophy, goals, and needs of the organization and the roles and responsibilities of RAs in mind.

Training can be offered at various times during the year and for various lengths of time. Preservice training in spring, fall, or both and inservice training throughout the year are very common. Preservice provides RAs with an opportunity to learn about their positions and the organization and to gain confidence in their own skills. Such training enables them to begin their jobs with core information and practice in skill areas. RAs trained prior to starting the job report less stress, more confidence in themselves, and a clearer conception of their responsibilities (Winston and Buckner, in press).

The model of choice for training involves intensive preservice training, preferably for academic credit. Preservice training should be directed at acquiring basic or core skills and knowledge that undergird the RA's role and responsibilities. Experience (Upcraft and Pilato, 1982) and research (Winston and Buckner, in press) confirm the superiority of preservice training in basic skills. Training in these areas while the RA is on the job is undercut by the RA's pressing need to deal with immediate problems; he or she is unable to concentrate on acquiring basic helping skills.

If the housing program subscribes to the student development philosophy defined earlier in this chapter, then a number of skills and a substantial amount of knowledge appear to be essential in preservice training. These skills and this knowledge include an understanding of the RA as peer helper and in other RA roles and responsibilities, the goals and philosophy of the housing program, and the concept of role modeling; an understanding of student development theory, especially as it applies to one's self; interpersonal and human relations skills, especially the ability to be an active listener and to give interchangeable responses (extensive supervised practice is necessary if trainees are to develop these skills to a functional level); an understanding of one's own values and of the values and attitudes of prominent subcultures or subpopulations within the residence hall population; informal needs-assessment techniques and goal-setting strategies; basic study skills; knowledge of campus and community services agencies and programs; and referral techniques and strategies. Other skills and areas of knowledge that preservice training can include are stress management (Schuele, 1982), assertiveness training (Darrah and Ochloch, 1982), conflict resolution (Kurtz and Albertus, 1974), and programming skills (Blimling and Miltenberger, 1981; Upcraft and Pilato, 1982). Preservice training that takes place just prior to the fall term should concentrate on the nuts and bolts of hall opening and operation, on procedures and rules, and on the development of working relationships among hall staffs and supervisors.

In-service training should take place throughout the academic year. An in-service program should respond to immediate concerns of both paraprofessionals and professionals, and it should be structured to provide alternative options based on interest, skill level, or special problems.

Although paraprofessional staff members may benefit personally from their jobs, studies have found that they can experience difficult job-related problems (Miller and Conyne, 1980). In a study of abuses encountered by RAs, Schuh and Shipton (1983) found that obscenities, sexual and racial slurs, malicious pranks, damage to personal property, harassment, and physical abuse were reported. While RAs may experience these external problems, the problems are more often internal; that is, stress, burnout, and personal problems may be higher in paraprofessional positions (Hornak, 1982; Miller and Conyne, 1980). Hornak (1982) suggests several reasons for RA burnout: the "fishbowl" existence, the long hours on alert for crisis intervention, role ambiguity, and expectations to discipline peers. In-service training and other staff activities must take these factors into account, and they should address them directly.

Supervision

Supervision requires commitment and sensitivity from RAs and their supervisors. RAs must balance a number of demands, and they cannot and should not devote full time or attention to the job. Because they are also maturing college students, their own developmental issues sometimes interfere with effective performance.

Problems of supervising often rest with supervisors. Because they are generally entry-level professionals whose experience in giving supervision and in receiving good supervision is limited, they are unsure of themselves and of how best to supervise RAs.

There are four different tacks that supervision can take. First, maternalistic supervision focuses on making the RA feel comfortable and happy. Little attention is paid to how well the RA functions in the hall; a friendly relationship is viewed as most important. Maternalistic supervisors feel a high need to be liked, so they tend to ignore unpleasant situations as long as possible, often until they get completely out of hand. This supervision style is generally characterized by cycles of crises. Second, authoritarian supervision keeps RAs on a short leash. This approach is based on a belief that RAs require constant attention, that they often need to be checked up on, and that they should be given very little authority. The supervisor, not the RA, makes the major decisions. This style, when practiced by a young professional, is often rooted in a desire to be seen in a favorable light by supervisors, and it reflects the professional's insecurity in the supervisory role. Third, laissez faire supervision encourages RAs to "do their own thing." RAs are told to come to the supervisor only if they cannot handle a problem. RAs are seldom given instructions on how to approach problems or on how to get things done. They are expected to find their own solutions, and they are led to believe that if they make mistakes they will bear the consequences alone. Problems are viewed as failures. Fourth, synergistic supervision, a cooperative endeavor that makes the total effect greater than the sum of effects taken independently, views the work of the RA as shared responsibilities. This approach to supervision places the emphasis both on the accomplishment of organizational goals and on the education and personal growth of individual RAs. Synergistic supervision requires education—RAs need to learn techniques for dealing effectively with residents, especially in helping and counseling relationships, in disciplinary situations, and in leading groups. Responsibilities and expectations need to be stated clearly—since RAs operate in a basically unstructured situation, they have nothing to guide them if they do not have a clear understanding of their roles and the goals of the housing program. Moreover, concern and support are essential as the RA deals with his or her own personal development. Supervisors need to understand how students, including RAs, develop and the issues that they typically face. Finally, both a clear statement of performance standards and frequent feedback, both positive and negative, are needed. Evaluations of performance are most helpful and effective when they are made immediately after the event that is being evaluated. In order for a synergistic approach to be effective, the RA and the supervisor must form and nurture a personal relationship characterized by mutual trust and respect. Effective supervisors have a clear understanding of the goal of the supervisory role and self-confidence that allows give-and-take in the relationship. A good supervisor is able to offer and accept constructive criticism that contributes to the RA's, as well as to his or her own growth (Delworth and others, 1974; Upcraft and Pilato, 1982).

Staff Evaluation Strategies

The first step in the evaluation process is to identify what should be evaluated. Delworth and others (1974) suggest five areas: fulfillment of job responsibilities; support, dedication and attitude issues; impact on residents and floor; creativity; and skill development. Information on these areas comes from a variety of sources: supervisors' observations, residents, other paraprofessionals, and individual self-reports.

It is difficult for supervisors to observe RAs in interactions with residents on their floors. However, supervisors can observe the attitudes, values, and skills of an individual's interactions with other staff members during staff training seminars and in personal contact with RAs. Residents can be valuable in providing constructive criticism and positive feedback if two conditions are met: Personal relationships (positive or negative) must not affect objective assessment, and residents must understand the RA's roles and responsibilities (Delworth and others, 1974). One common technique is for residents to complete standardized instruments anonymously. These instruments usually take the form of organization-specific questionnaires developed by the professional staff. A third source of information is other paraprofessionals. Group meetings are one appropriate technique for gathering such information. While group evaluation meetings can be viewed as a threat or cause tension, warm, positive, and caring facilitation can enable staff members to learn from one another. The final source is the individual RAs. A challenging and supportive environment, a caring supervisor, established goals, and appropriate evaluation measures assist RAs in assessing their strengths and weaknesses and in making plans for improvement. Evaluation information should be used to assist paraprofessionals in their own development.

Innovative Uses of Paraprofessionals in Residence Halls

Resident Assistants in a Living Learning Center. The Collins Living Learning Center (LLC) is a residential complex at Indiana University. It houses 550 undergraduate and graduate students. The LLC is staffed by a director, a coordinator of residence life, an assistant coordinator, a faculty member-in-residence, and student paraprofessionals, who are referred to as resident fellows (RFs). Resident fellows have responsibilities similar to those of resident assistants in many housing programs.

The LLC was established to provide students with a residential facility and staff that could complement students' academic experience by integrating learning experiences involving the classroom and the residence community. It is organized around numerous student governing and programming boards that have created a dynamic residential curriculum. The LLC curriculum has four guiding principles: first, to foster a liberal and integral style of learning among students; second, to encourage interdisciplinary exchange and cross-fertilization of ideas; third, to endow the student's social life with an intellectual basis and interpersonal context for academic dialogue; and fourth, to help make learning cooperative and participatory by giving students a voice in curriculum decision making and an opportunity to teach and learn from one another as well as from academic specialists. The center's programming includes such activities as an artist-in-residence program, a distinguished visitors program, receptions for artists and public figures, dinner forums, faculty lunches, language tables, theater/opera nights, sponsored trips to special events and exhibits, performing arts productions, and film series.

Each residence unit within the LLC is served by a resident fellow. RFs are half-time employees of the Department of Residence Life, and they are expected to assist with the administrative operation of the center, enforce university and residence life regulations, communicate information about university services and resources, and implement education, cultural, social, and recreational programs. In addition, the RF fulfills a number of group advising roles, academic advising functions, and tutoring. For example, RFs are expected to advise three LLC clubs, organizations, programming boards, or major student projects in addition to their own residence unit government; act as a tutor for students in their academic major or area of special competence; conduct or organize at least one center and two floor unit academic programs each semester, such as a free class, round table discussion, speaker series, reading, writing, or public speaking groups, or study skills assistance; and participate in the center's one-hour credit course, "Residential Learning Workshop," required of all incoming students.

Resident Assistants as Facilitators of Student Development Programming. The University of Wisconsin–Stevens Point is a state institution enrolling approximately 8,300 students. The residence halls accommodate about 3,500 student in both single-sex and coeducational facilities. The mission of the residence life program reflects a commitment to create opportunities for students to engage in holistic developmental growth-producing experiences. This mission is carried out in part through the promotion and development of wellness programming in the residence halls. The focus of this programming is to assist students in taking responsibility for their own growth and development in the six dimensions of wellness: social, occupational, spiritual, physical, intellectual, and emotional.

The RA position includes responsibilities in counseling, academic advising, programming, disciplining, and providing resources. To help the RAs to become effective student development agents, they are encouraged to achieve seven personal and organizational goals: first, to grow personally and share themselves with others; second, to challenge and encourage students to set goals in each of the six wellness dimensions; third, to offer students feedback and receive feedback from students regarding positive and negative behaviors or reexamination of personal goals; fourth, to offer alternatives to students that may help them attain a goal or solve a problem; fifth, to encourage community involvement and the sharing of ideas and talents; sixth, to communicate and develop educational resources that students can use in their academic planning and goal setting; and seventh, to help each student recognize his or her uniqueness.

Generally, the RA position is looked on favorably by students, supervising personnel, and professional administrative staff. One recurring organizational management challenge is to maintain a high-quality paraprofessional program within a system that encourages supervisory autonomy, community uniqueness, and individualized creative programming. Also, at a number of halls, other student programming paraprofessionals, called such things as *lifestyle assistants* and *student reaction teams,* work in the hall with the RAs. Keeping roles and responsibilities clearly defined among these positions requires continuing effort.

References

American College Personnel Association. "Statement of Ethical and Professional Standards." *Journal of College Student Personnel,* 1981, *22,* 184–189.

Atkinson, D. R., Williams, R. D., and Garb, E. "The Personal Orientation Inventory as a Predictor of Resident Assistant Effectiveness." *Journal of College Student Personnel,* 1973, *14,* 326–332.

Blimling, G. S., and Miltenberger, L. J. *The Resident Assistant: Working with College Students in Residence Halls.* Dubuque, Iowa: Kendall/Hunt, 1981.

Brown, R. D. "Student Development and the Academy: New Directions and Horizons." In D. A. DeCoster and P. Mable (Eds.), *Personal Education and Community Development in College Residence Halls.* Washington, D.C.: American College Personnel Association, 1980.

Bumba, R. P., Jr., Heyl, R. W., Miller, A. G., and Schuh, J. H. "Staff Selection and Training: Can the Two Functions Be Combined? *Journal of College and University Student Housing,* 1980, *10* (1), 20–24.

Cannon, J. R., and Peterman, J. G. "Functional Selection Indexes for Residence Hall Advisors." *Journal of College Student Personnel.* 1973, *14.* 549.

Darrah, P. E., and Ochloch, S. K. "A Program in Assertion Training for College Students." *Journal of College Student Personnel,* 1982, *23* (5), 443–445.

DeCoster, D. A., and Mable, P. "Residence Education: Purpose and Process." In D. A. DeCoster and P. Mable (Eds.), *Personal Education and Community Development in College Residence Halls.* Washington, D.C.: American College Personnel Association, 1980.

Delworth, U., Sherwood, G., and Casaburri, N. *Student Paraprofessionals: A Working Model for Higher Education.* Washington, D.C.: American Personnel and Guidance Association, 1974.

German, S. C. "Selecting Undergraduate Paraprofessionals on College Campuses: A Review." *Journal of College Student Personnel,* 1979, *20,* 28–34.

Greenleaf, E. D. "The Role of Student Staff Members." In D. A. DeCoster and P. Mable (Eds.), *Student Development and Education in College Residence Halls.* Washington, D.C.: American Personnel and Guidance Association, 1974.

Hall, M., and Creed, W. "The Use of the CPI in the Evaluation and Selection of Resident Assistants." *Journal of College and University Student Housing,* 1979, *9* (1), 10–13.

Hornak, J. "Resident Assistant Burnout: A Self-Defeating Behavior." *Journal of College and University Student Housing*, 1982, *12*, 14–16.

Klockars, A. J., and Walkup, H. R. "The PRF and Peer Ratings." *Educational and Psychological Measurement*, 1980, *40*, 1,099–1,103.

Kipp, D. J. "The Personal Orientation Inventory: A Predictive Device for Resident Advisors." *Journal of College Student Personnel*, 1979, *20*, 382–384.

Kurtz, R. R., and Albertus, A. "A Workshop for Residence Assistants on Inter-personal Conflict and Third-Party Consultation." *Journal of College and University Student Housing*, 1974, *4* (2), 26–29.

Mable, P., and DeCoster, D. A. "The Role of Students as Staff Members." In D. A. DeCoster and P. Mable (Eds.), *Personal Education and Community Development in College Residence Halls*. Washington, D.C.: American College Personnel Association, 1980.

Miller, C. J., and Conyne, R. K. "Paraprofessional Problems: A Comparison of Residence Hall Paraprofessionals and Regular Students." *Journal of College and University Student Housing*, 1980, *10* (1), 10–12.

Miller, T. K., and Prince, J. S. *The Future of Student Affairs: A Guide to Student Development for Tomorrow's Higher Education*. San Francisco: Jossey-Bass, 1976.

Moore, D. R., and Murray, L. "Torts: Your Legal Duties and Responsibilities." In D. D. Gehring (Ed.), *Administering College and University Housing: A Legal Perspective*. Asheville, N.C.: College Administration Publications, 1983.

Morton, L. J. "The CPI: Significance as a Resident Assistant Selection Aid." *Journal of College and University Student Housing*, 1975–1976, *5* (2), 16–21.

Murphy, R. O., and Ortenzi, A. "Use of Standardized Instruments in the Selection of Residence Hall Staff." *Journal of College Student Personnel*, 1966, *7*, 360–363.

Newton, F. B. "The Effect of Systematic Communication Skills Training on Residence Hall Paraprofessionals." *Journal of College Student Personnel*, 1974, *15*, 366–369.

Pavela, G. "Constitutional Issues in the Residence Halls." In D. D. Gehring (Ed.), *Administering College and University Housing: A Legal Perspective*. Asheville, N.C.: College Administration Publications, 1983.

Riker, H. C., and DeCoster, D. A. "The Educational Role in College Student Housing," *Journal of College and University Student Housing*, 1971, *1* (1), 1–4.

Schroeder, C. C., and Wills, B. S. "An Attempt to Use a Measure of Self-Actualization in the Selection of Resident Assistants." *Journal of College and University Student Housing*, 1973, *3* (1), 30–32.

Schuele, M. K. "A Stress Management Workshop for Residence Hall Staff." *Journal of College Student Personnel*, 1982, *23*, 84.

Schuh, J. H., and Shipton, W. C. "Abuses Encountered by Resident Assistants During an Academic Year." *Journal of College Student Personnel*, 1983, *24*, 428–432.

Scroggins, W. F., and Ivey, A. E. "Teaching and Maintaining Microcounseling Skills with a Residence Hall Staff." *Journal of College Student Personnel*, 1978, *19*, 158–162.

Tibbits, S. "Student Staff Selection: Peer Evaluation May Be Best." *NASPA Journal*, 1977, *14*, 65-68.

Upcraft, M. L., and Pilato, G. T. *Residence Hall Assistants in College: A Guide to Selection, Training, and Supervision*. San Francisco: Jossey-Bass, 1982.

Winston, R. B., Jr., and Buckner, J. D. "The Effects of Peer Helper Training and Timing of Training on Resident Assistants' Reported Stress." *Journal of College Student Personnel*, in press.

Zunker, V. G., and Brown, W. F. "Comparative Effectiveness of Student and Professional Counselors." *Personnel and Guidance Journal*, 1966, *44*, 738–743.

Roger B. Winston, Jr., is associate professor in the Department of Counseling and Human Development Services, College of Education, University of Georgia. He has directed a residence hall program, and he currently teaches in the resident assistant training program.

Marcy S. Ullom is administrative assistant in the Department of University Housing at the University of Georgia. A former area coordinator, she has conducted research on residence hall programs, and she teaches in the resident assistant training program.

Charles J. Werring is assistant director of residence life at Texas Tech University, where he has overall responsibility for residence hall programs, including resident assistants. He has been active in the American College Personnel Association Commission III and in the Association of College and University Housing Officers.

Student paraprofessionals are an integral part of the orientation process for new students.

Orientation and the Role of the Student Paraprofessional

Kenneth L. Ender
Gerry Strumpf

The use of paraprofessional staff is becoming increasingly important to the success of new student orientation programs. In a recent survey of 353 institutions of higher education, more than 50 percent reported using either paid or volunteer students as staff for the program (National Orientation Directors Association Data Bank, 1982). In another study, 90 percent of the institutions surveyed reported using undergraduates in their orientation programs (Staudenmeir and Marchetti, 1983). This chapter presents a contemporary perspective on orientation, discusses the appropriate roles and job functions for professionals and paraprofessionals in the orientation setting, describes a systematic approach for the development of orientation programs that use paraprofessionals, and outlines two exemplary approaches using paraprofessionals in student orientation.

New Student Orientation: A Contemporary Perspective

In recently adopted standards for orientation programs (Council for the Advancement of Standards, 1983), the stated mission of orientation is to provide ongoing services and assistance that will aid new students in their

S. Ender, R. Winston (Eds.). *Using Students as Paraprofessional Staff.* New Directions for Student Services, no. 27. San Francisco: Jossey-Bass, September 1984.

transition to the institution, expose new students to the broad educational opportunities provided by the institution, and integrate new students into the life of the institution.

As institutions of higher education focus increasingly on retention, successful orientation efforts are being viewed as the first step in a comprehensive retention program. A recent study reported that "the group of eight institutions that had the most comprehensive orientation and advising program showed that an average of 60 percent of the full-time freshmen graduate in two to five years, while a group of sixteen institutions with the least comprehensive program had a persistence rate of 14 percent" (Forrest, 1982, p. 28).

The Council for Advancement of Standards (1983) has postulated these eighteen goals for a successful orientation program:

- To assist students in understanding the purpose of higher education in general
- To assist students in understanding the mission of the specific institution
- To assist students in developing an identity and a relationship with the institution, peers, staff, and community
- To establish the institution's expectations of students
- To provide information and self-assessment measurements that help students to understand the level of competition and their own competitive posture
- To identify costs of attending the institution, in terms of both dollars and personal commitment
- To improve the retention rate of new students
- To provide an atmosphere and sufficient information to enable students to make reasoned and well-informed choices
- To provide information concerning academic policies, procedures, and programs
- To promote an awareness of nonclassroom opportunities
- To provide qualified counseling and advising
- To explain the process for class scheduling and registration and provide trained, supportive assistance to accomplish these tasks
- To develop familiarity with the physical surroundings
- To provide information and exposure to available school services
- To help students identify and evaluate living and commuting options
- To create an atmosphere that minimizes anxiety, promotes positive attitudes, and stimulates an environment for learning
- To provide appropriate information on personal safety and security
- To provide current student contact to discuss new students' expectations and continuing students' perceptions of the campus.

These goals are comprehensive. They provide a framework for program planning and assessment. Moreover, they can be used to develop insight into the potential roles and responsibilities of both professional and paraprofessional staff, regardless of the orientation model chosen.

Orientation Models

There are three primary models in contemporary orientation programs: freshmen week, summer programs, and ongoing orientation during the freshman year.

Freshmen Week. Freshmen week is typically held four to five days before fall class registration. Freshmen week programs focus primarily on assisting new students as they become acquainted with one another, on orienting new students to campus services and resources, and on providing academic planning and preliminary course scheduling. This model is the least comprehensive orientation approach, and its limitations become particularly obvious if it stands by itself as an orientation tool.

Summer Program. Summer programs ranging in length from one to four days are increasingly being reported as a model for orientation (National Orientation Directors Association Data Bank, 1982). Typically much more comprehensive than the freshmen week programs, the summer programs are usually repeated throughout the summer months so that small groups of new students can receive an introduction to campus life that addresses policies, procedures, and institutional expectations. The primary focus of these programs is on small-group interaction, academic planning, and first-term course selection. They also help students to become familiar with campus surroundings and student support services.

Ongoing Programs. Ongoing programs are usually paired with a freshmen week or with a summer program. As a result, the ongoing program is the most comprehensive model. Ongoing programs view orientation as an ongoing process and design the program to match new students' first-term experience. Such programs focus on academic and career planning, on teaching students how to use campus resources, and on helping students to develop interpersonal skills.

Paraprofessional and Professional Roles in Orientation

Regardless of the orientation model chosen, paraprofessionals can play an important and integral part. Distinguishing appropriate roles and responsibilities for the paraprofessional and the professional is an important first step in program planning.

Professional Roles. Most orientation programs in this country rely heavily on student paraprofessionals to enhance their effectiveness. However, some tasks require direct leadership and involvement from a professional staff member.

Program Leadership. Responsibility for the development of orientation at four-year institutions is usually coordinated by the office of the dean of students. At community colleges, programming is most often provided by the counseling service (Van Eaton, 1972). Administrative units that have primary responsibility for directing orientation programs include the assistant dean of students, the dean of student affairs, or the director of student activities (Staudenmeir and Marchetti, 1983). At many institutions, program leadership is the responsibility of a staff member who has an orientation title, such as *director of orientation, coordinator of orientation,* or *director of new student programs*) (Staudenmeir and Marchetti, 1983). The responsibilities of the program leader include articulating program philosophy, creating goals and objectives, determining budget, and conducting evaluation (Packwood, 1977).

Publication Development. Designing a communicative tool that effectively markets the goals of an orientation program is critical to the program's success, and it is a task for the professional. Successful orientation programs provide orientation materials that are carefully prepared and presented (Kramer and Washburn, 1982). New students look on the published materials as evidence that the institution has an awareness of their pre-entry needs.

Selection and Training of Paraprofessional Staff. Selection and training of paraprofessional staff are extremely important responsibilities. The selection process is critical to program success. The composition of the group that chooses the paraprofessionals requires careful attention. Faculty, staff, and former paraprofessionals are generally included. The professional staff member must work to ensure that the selection group reflects an adequate mix of gender and race. As Packwood (1977) has noted, the second consideration is extremely important. The professional must also ensure that the selection group has a clear understanding of the selection criteria. These criteria typically include the applicant's leadership experience and style, knowledge of the institution, interpersonal skills, and academic ability (Delworth and others, 1974).

The professional's next critical role involves training. The competence of paraprofessional staff is critical to the success and integrity of a paraprofessional-staffed orientation program. Training typically addresses three areas: knowledge of the institution and its resources, interpersonal and group skills, and any special skills required for specific program components, such as audiovisual services and public speaking (Packwood, 1977).

Program Evaluation. Program evaluation also requires professional leadership. The evaluation process typically involves input from all program participants—paraprofessional staff, administrative staff, faculty, new students, and new students' parents. Evaluation should measure the program's policies and procedures, assess the effectiveness of staff, and provide information about the program's impact on new students (Barr and others, 1979). Successful evaluation efforts by the professional provide a starting point for future orientation program planning.

Paraprofessional Role. The other components of the orientation program are best responded to by paraprofessionals. Successful matching of program goals and objectives with paraprofessionals' skills and interests helps to identify these components. In determining the appropriate role for paraprofessionals, it is critical to match their skills with specific programmatic tasks. The paragraphs that follow describe possible objectives for the paraprofessional role.

Trained upperclass paraprofessionals can provide a forum in which new students can share their perspectives and concerns. One of the primary strengths of an effective orientation program lies in personalization of the institution for new students. New students are like aliens traveling a foreign land who have no understanding of its mores and customs. While professional staff may understand the new student's plight, they are not always able to identify with the new student's fears and concerns. Adequately trained paraprofessionals can not only identify with new students but give them helpful survival tips based on their own experience. Paraprofessionals are an important link with new students as they travel in this new land.

Paraprofessionals can provide new students with an overall introduction to the institution's support services and to its academic policies and procedures. Paraprofessionals can be trained to communicate the internal workings of the institution to new students, and they can explain the use of such resource materials as catalogues and class schedules. Such communication can take place in individual interviews or in small-group sessions. Paraprofessionals can describe academic requirements as well as the support services that are available to new students.

Paraprofessionals can provide new students with a physical orientation to the institution. Paraprofessionals can conduct the campus tour. They can point out buildings where specific services are housed, and they can be trained to give new students a perspective on the institution that is both contemporary and historically based. Important traditions, mores, and customs can be communicated effectively by paraprofessionals in this setting.

Paraprofessionals can serve as an information and referral agent for new students. One of the major advantages of a paraprofessional program is that it allows the orientation process to be personalized. Paraprofessionals can use their own unique perspectives to identify the various resources and services that individual new students will need.

Finally, paraprofessionals can develop a class schedule for the immediate term and help students to understand its relationship to future schedules and plans. Many orientation programs include advisement and registration for first-term classes (National Orientation Directors Association Data Bank, 1982). At some institutions, paraprofessionals are trained to provide new students with academic advising. Most campuses, however, use faculty or professional advisors for the advising task. On these campuses, paraprofessionals can help students to develop a class schedule from the courses that were advised by the professional.

Expanded Paraprofessional Roles. As orientation programs become increasingly ongoing in nature, the role of paraprofessionals is expanding. The paragraphs in this section describe some examples of paraprofessional roles and functions in the continuing orientation process.

Peer Facilitators in Orientation Courses. At Bentley College in Massachusetts, paraprofessionals are used as facilitators in introductory orientation courses (Austin, 1984). In this program, paraprofessionals help to develop the group support system, discuss common personal development issues, and assist students in skill development areas.

Big Brother/Big Sister. Many institutions across the country have recognized that one of the chief factors in retention of students occurs within the first three weeks of classes. The University of Tennessee and the University of Maryland have developed big brother/big sister programs designed specifically to assist students during their first month on campus. Paraprofessionals are used in these programs to assist students personally with registration, to prepare students for their first day of class, to provide freshmen with a personal contact on admission, and to help new students become active and participating members in the university community (Schriver, 1984; Strumpf, 1984).

Peer Support. One primary goal of the peer support programs that have been developed by orientation offices is to provide new students with personal support during their first year. Generally, paraprofessional contacts identify high-risk students, whom paraprofessionals assist with both personal and academic adjustment through individual interviews. At the University of Tennessee, such a program has been found to be extremely useful in establishing peer support systems and personalizing the campus environment (Schriver, 1984).

Commuter Assistants. At Virginia Commonwealth University, paraprofessionals are used in continuing orientation programs as commuter assistants (Ender, 1984). The commuter assistant works in an ongoing fashion with commuter students. Typically, assignments are made at the first orientation session, and commuter assistants work with the new commuter student during the first year or first term. Their primary responsibilities are usually personal acquaintance and institutional affiliation. The typical activities of commuter assistants in continuing orientation programs include identification of institutional resources, campus activities, car pools and mass transit, and making new friends.

Developing a Paraprofessional Orientation Program

Institutional Readiness. Several key variables need to be assessed when determining an institution's readiness to use student paraprofessionals in orientation programs. These variables include the current level of paraprofessional involvement on campus; students' representation in campus governance policy decisions; the level of student, faculty, and staff involvement in decision making and problem solving; and the availability of faculty and campus staff skilled in teaching leadership, interpersonal, and helping skills.

While the assessment does not have to be affirmative for all these variables, program designers should assess the institution's readiness in these areas before suggesting student involvement in orientation programs. For students to work successfully in this setting, a solid partnership among faculty, staff, and students needs to be formed before actual delivery of the program begins. Program designers who are attempting to be successful by accomplishing the eighteen goals set out earlier in this chapter need not prove that students are capable of working in the setting once the program is under way. The key to determining institutional readiness for the use of paraprofessionals in an orientation program is acceptance of students as competent program partners by faculty and staff.

Student Readiness. Student readiness must also be assessed. The important variables that need to be considered are the level of student leadership on campus; students' readiness to receive training in interpersonal, leadership, and helping skills; students' interest in becoming involved; the need for financial remuneration to motivate students; and the level of students' satisfaction with the institution (there are always some negative issues in an academic setting).

Program designers should be aware that new students are more ready to trust student paraprofessionals' perceptions of campus life than they are to trust written materials or staff and faculty presentations. It is extremely important for paraprofessionals to represent the entire campus scene.

Essential Components of Paraprofessional Orientation Programs

Preemployment Activities. Developing a candidate pool that matches the demographic characteristics of new students is essential to the program's success. Since paraprofessionals are extremely helpful in assisting new students to determine whether they fit the institution, the student staff should in some way mirror the new students. Careful attention to such demographics on new students as gender, ethnicity, housing, age, and choice of schools and majors is essential.

Assessing the knowledge that potential paraprofessionals have about campus is essential during the recruitment phase of the program. While it is not particularly important for paraprofessionals to be hired for what they know, their supervisors should be aware of what they do not know.

Recruiting Orientation Paraprofessionals. The recruitment of orientation paraprofessionals begins by developing an appropriate program description with corresponding candidate qualifications and corresponding position descriptions. Whether paraprofessionals work for pay or volunteer their services, they must have a clear understanding of the job's duties and of the expected qualifications.

Most orientation programs are fast-paced and vigorous, and student staff have multiple responsibilities. It is therefore important for student staff to demonstrate an ability to work under pressure, to connect with a diversity of people, to communicate enthusiasm and acceptance of others, and to be able to work successfully as part of a team. While it is difficult to determine in advance whether a candidate has these qualities, some approaches have been successful. Candidates' abilities can be assessed by conducting a preemployment workshop for all interested candidates. The workshop must be designed to be fast-paced, rigorous, slightly risky interpersonally, and fun. It must attempt to replicate the whole orientation experience on a very small scale. Immediately after the workshop, staff members record their observations of participating students, including their interaction and participation. These data are used to determine whom to invite for the formal interviews.

Selection. Selection represents the final phase of preemployment. Where possible, faculty and staff involved in implementation of the program should take part so as to ensure institutional commitment and support for the student staff. The selection process should attempt to measure the applicants' writing and speaking skills, their willingness and capability to work in a team environment, and their understanding of basic institutional information. The preemployment workshop just described can assist in measuring speaking skills and willingness or potential to work as a team member. Writing skills and knowledge of the university community can easily be assessed through application materials and through the use of a short-answer, true-or-false, multiple-choice quiz about the institution. By using these types of activities together with personal interviews, it becomes possible to select a competent student staff.

Training Programs. The selection process can be effective in selecting potentially good orientation paraprofessionals, but training is essential to ensure that undergraduates can effectively represent the institution in a positive and honest manner to new students and their parents. Often, the content of the training program is dictated by the design of the specific orientation session. However, any well-developed training program should address certain general areas: knowledge of self, communication and group facilitation skills, knowledge of campus, and knowledge of orientation consumers.

In the area of knowledge of self, the training program should include a section that helps paraprofessionals to clarify and understand their values, attitudes, strengths, and weaknesses. Training in this area should stress the paraprofessionals' ability to work in a team and with the variety of students who attend the orientation program. In the area of communication and group facilitation skills, paraprofessionals in orientation need effective listening skills, presentation and public speaking skills, assertiveness, group facilitation, and decision-making strategies. The knowledge of campus area focuses on paraprofessionals' understanding of academic policies and procedures, the institution's structure, and its support services and resources. In the area of knowledge of consumers, paraprofessionals should have a good working knowledge of the different populations with which they will work. This list might include freshmen, transfer students, graduate students, parents, minority students, older returning students, and commuter or resident students.

There are many different models for providing orientation paraprofessionals with training. These models range from full-credit academic courses to intensive one- or two-week sessions prior to the orientation program. Of the 353 institutions that participated in the 1982 National Orientation Directors Association Survey, 53 (15 percent) had credit-bearing courses, while the rest used non-credit-bearing training sessions (National Orientation Directors Association, 1982). There are four common approaches to training: academic courses, ongoing non-academic-credit seminars, one- or two-week programs, and retreats. Many programs combine two or more of these approaches to carry out the specified goals of their training program. The first and most important step in designing the training program is a well-defined statement of purpose. Once the purpose and goals have been delineated, appropriate training options can be developed.

Academic Courses. Academic courses have several advantages: They allow a great deal of time to be spent on training paraprofessionals over an extended period of time, academic credit eliminates the need for other reward systems, and a variety of teaching approaches can be used to enhance the training experience. This approach also has some disadvantages. Applicants may not have time to include an additional course, academic plans may not allow the credit to be applied to degree requests, and applicants who are not able to take a credit-bearing class will be at a disadvantage when competing for the orientation job.

Ongoing Non-Academic-Credit Seminars. Ongoing non-academic-credit seminars have much the same training focus as academic courses and many of the same advantages. However, with non-credit-bearing seminars, it is very important for the trainer to build in a reward system for the time that paraprofessionals devote to training. The reward may come in the form of monetary compensation or of a certificate indicating that the possessor has received a specified number of hours of leadership training.

One- or Two-Week Programs. One- or two-week programs focus primarily on skill development, on developing knowledge about the institution, and on team building. One clear advantage of this training approach is that paraprofessional staff will retain the institutional information for immediate transmission to new students. Two primary disadvantages of this model are that it does not encourage self-awareness and that group cohesiveness will not be as great due to the program's short duration.

Retreats. Intense retreats are quite helpful preceding a longer training model, such as a course or seminar, and they can focus directly on self-assessment, program goal development, and team building.

Maintaining Paraprofessionals Through the Program. Program implementation is typically high-pressure and fast-paced. Supervision and support of student staff are essential for program success.

Individual Supervision. Each student staff member should begin the program with personal goals and objectives, which should be shared with the supervisor and other paraprofessional staff members (Delahunty and others, 1983). Ideally, these goals and objectives are developed at some point within the training, and they serve as a focus for supervision and support for paraprofessionals as the program unfolds. It is important for the paraprofessionals' goals and objectives to relate to the position description, to staff development goals, and to their own personal development goals. In this way, evaluation can be comprehensive.

While a weekly individual meeting with each student staff member is ideal, it is often impossible because of the sheer numbers of student staff and program commitments. Each paraprofessional should participate in a minimum of three one-on-one meetings with the supervisor before the program ends. One session should be held before the program begins to discuss and design personal goals and objectives. A mid program session should review progress, modify or change goals and objectives, and provide support. The last session should evaluate the paraprofessional's performance and success in achieving the stated objectives.

While it is difficult to meet individually with student staff members, it is both convenient and critical to conduct group supervision meetings on a weekly basis. These group meetings should be used to evaluate staff effectiveness and to provide a forum at which individuals can share feedback with student and staff team members. As the program unfolds, these group meetings provide excellent opportunities for staff to release anxieties, tensions, and apprehensions and to support fellow team members as they attempt to meet their personal objectives.

Evaluation. Evaluation of the program should parallel individual and program goals. It is critical to the ongoing success of efforts to use paraprofessionals for student staff to be evaluated by all program participants. Evaluation instruments completed by new students, their parents, faculty participants, and fellow staff members should ask questions related to paraprofessionals' effectiveness. A self-evaluation instrument for paraprofessionals is an effective device for individual evaluation.

Paraprofessionals in Student Orientation:
Two Exemplary Programs

The use of student paraprofessionals in new student orientation programs is strongly supported nationally. Used primarily to personalize the environment and to assist faculty and staff in providing institutional support systems, paraprofessionals are useful in a variety of models to provide comprehensive new student orientation. The success of paraprofessional programs depends heavily on forming a good partnership with faculty and staff colleagues, on sound and reasonable position descriptions, on effective training, and on timely supervision and support. Two exemplary programs are models of such programming efforts.

Bentley College Freshmen Seminar Program. The most formalized means of providing an ongoing orientation program at Bentley College is FS101, the Freshmen Seminar Course. The program has six goals: to assist students in developing an awareness of Bentley College resources and of the ways in which they can be used to enhance their academic experience; to expand the educational orientation of students through an understanding of the learning process and the integration of various disciplines into a program of study; to assist students in assessing their goals, values, and skills in relation to personal, educational, and career development; to complement the academic advising system by providing a format that allows the advisor-advisee relationship to develop; to increase students' interpersonal and communication skills through a variety of small-group experiences; and to improve the retention rate among new students by decreasing their sense of anomie and by developing their feelings of affiliation, competence, and purpose.

The course was piloted in fall 1982, when five sections were offered. Each section was facilitated by a faculty member, a staff member, and an orientation paraprofessional. The faculty member was the academic adviser assigned to the twenty students in each section. Paraprofessionals helped to facilitate the group support system, discussed common personal development issues, and assisted students in skill development areas.

Orientation at Bradley University. Paraprofessional orientation leaders serve in the Student Aide Services at Bradley University. They help to acclimate entering and returning students to the campus by developing, initiating, and promoting programs that meet students' academic, social, and career exploration needs. Student aides achieve these goals through summer orientation and in four ongoing school-year programs: FOOTSTEPS, Tutor File, Bradley Connection, and Health Education.

New aides are hired in February, and they serve as apprentices to graduating student aides in order to learn the responsibilities of the school-year programs. "Cookbooks" specifying instructions for successful programming are passed down from year to year for each program. Further training throughout the spring semester includes weekly meetings with department chairmen, who explain criteria for class scheduling and placement. Each aide is assigned to a college within the university and becomes responsible for providing academic advising to students in that college during the summer orientation program.

Another week-long basic training program takes place just prior to the start of summer orientation. To gain a comprehensive understanding of the university, the aides meet with administrators, who range from the director of food service to the president of the university. Communication skills and counseling techniques are also taught by counseling center personnel during this time.

During each of the twelve, three-day summer orientation sessions, new students meet their academic adviser, preregister for classes, learn their way around campus, and meet approximately seventy-five other entering students. The aides help the new students to adjust to college life by conducting individual and group appointments with the entering freshmen. The aides answer questions and alleviate concerns by offering knowledge based on actual experience and training. The aides also help new students to select classes, and they plan, organize, and supervise the social activities during each session. The aides proctor placement tests and evaluations during the summer sessions. The aides also facilitate discussions that provide insight into campus life at Bradley, and they participate in question-and-answer periods to alleviate the concerns of parents. The orientation program offers a taste of college life to entering students and parents.

During the academic year, the student aide coordinator and the student aides report to the director of educational development. The role of the synergistic team is carried into the semester. Each student aide is assigned one of the four ongoing school year programs.

FOOTSTEPS is a career exploration program that gives students an opportunity to investigate and test career interests by visiting with a professional for a portion of his or her working day. Career interests are tested by the Human Evaluation Center, and test results are combined with information sheets to discover career interests. The aides match students with FOOTSTEP volunteer companies, whose participation is solicited by telephone, mail, and speaking engagements.

Tutor File is a computer listing of academic tutors. Students in need of academic assistance are given a computer list of qualified tutors. Potential tutors complete an application identifying the classes that they are qualified to tutor, their price per hour, and their telephone number; applications must have an endorsing signature from the appropriate professor. Aides assist students as they interact with this program.

Bradley Connection, the student contact outreach program, provides information to prospective students. The aides and the admissions office work together to organize and contact each admitted student for the upcoming year via telephone and mail correspondence. More than 225 volunteers contact more than 1,200 students throughout the year.

The health center and the aides form the Health Education program. The aides organize and publicize lectures on such health-related topics as anorexia nervosa and bulimia, birth control, and stress management.

The positive impact of these programs can be quantified. The Evaluative Survey Service (ESS), a campus climate study sponsored by the American College Testing (ACT) program, identified the summer orientation program as the single most positive aspect of the Bradley campus. Faculty who were wary of involving students in the class-scheduling process find that the aides' work is flawless. Faculty note that assistance from aides gives them time in which to discuss more substantive issues with students. Evaluations by entering students indicate that the student aides made their transition to college easier. This judgment is underlined by the freshmen- to sophomore-year retention rate of 86 percent. It is clear that a well-trained paraprofessional staff is an important part of enrollment management at one institution.

References

Austin, Diane. Personal communication, January 1984.

Barr, M. J., Justice, S. H., and Young, B. D. "Orientation." In G. D. Kuh (Ed.), *Evaluation in Student Affairs.* Carbondale, Ill.: American College Personnel Association, 1979.

Council for the Advancement of Standards. *Standards for Orientation.* 1983.

Delahunty, T. M., Eisenberg, M. S., and Ender, K. L. "SOAR: A Strategy for Student Development." *National Orientation Directors Association Journal,* spring 1983, *1* (2), 3–12.

Delworth, U., Sherwood, G. and Casaburri, N. *Student Paraprofessionals: A Working Model for Higher Education.* Washington, D.C.: American College Personnel Association, 1974.

Ender, K. L. Personal communication, January, 1984.

Forrest, A. *Increasing Student Competence and Persistence.* Iowa City: American College Testing Program, 1982.

Kramer, L. G., and Washburn, R. "The Perceived Orientation Needs of New Students." *Journal of College Student Personnel,* 1982, *24,* 311–319.

Packwood, W. T. *College Student Personnel Services.* Springfield, Ill.: Thomas, 1977.

National Orientation Directors Association Data Bank, *Handbook for Orientation Directors.* 1982.

Schriver, D. Personal communication, January 1984.

Staudenmeir, J., and Marchetti, J. J. "Orientation Programs and Practices: 1963–1981." *National Orientation Directors Journal,* fall 1983, *2* (1), 9–15.

Strumpf, G. Personal communication, January 1984.

Van Eaton, E. N. "National Study of Trends in Orientation." *The National Orientation,* 1972, *2* (4), 3.

Kenneth L. Ender is director of student activities and of the university student commons at Virginia Commonwealth University. His office shares institutional responsibility for the Summer Orientation, Advising, and Registration Program (SOAR).

Gerry Strumpf is director of orientation at the University of Maryland, College Park. A former member of the board of directors for the National Orientation Directors Association (NODA), she now serves as editor of the NODA Data Bank and as the NODA voting delegate to the Council for Advancement of Standards.

*Student paraprofessionals have found a solid home in
counseling and career functions. Increased use of technology
and structured groups in these agencies shows that use of
paraprofessionals is increasing.*

Student Paraprofessionals in Counseling and Career Centers

*Ursula Delworth
Mary Johnson*

Paraprofessional programs in counseling and career centers appear to be a
growth industry, which has been fueled by recent advances in technology and
by increased use of structured groups to deliver services to students. In a
recent survey (Salovey, 1983), 122 counseling centers (of the 156 respondents) reported using peer counselors. Functions ranged from residence hall
counseling and advising (79 percent) and tutoring (62 percent) to counseling
of returning students (1 percent) and student ambulance/Emergency Medi-
cal Technician work (1 percent). It is worthy to note that 24 percent of the
centers reported using paraprofessionals for suicide and crisis intervention
and general psychological counseling and that 35 percent used peers in
career guidance services. Ender and Winston (1984) report that 34.5 percent
of the counseling centers and 32.9 percent of the career centers that they
surveyed were using student paraprofessionals. Clearly, counseling and
career centers are not the largest users of paraprofessional personnel, but the
numbers are solid, and the programs are well established and creative.

Use of student paraprofessionals in counseling and career work is
mainly a phenomenon of the 1970s. Fifteen years ago, counseling personnel
were often involved as trainers and advisors to the vast array of peer help
groups and hot lines that students initiated on campuses across the country.

S. Ender, R. Winston (Eds.). *Using Students as Paraprofessional Staff.* New
Directions for Student Services, no. 27. San Francisco: Jossey-Bass, September 1984.

As such groups died away in the mid and late 1970s, professionals who had observed that peers could be useful moved to incorporate services by student paraprofessionals into professional agencies. The work of Carkhuff (1969) and others demonstrated that paraprofessionals could be trained to offer effective helping services, and it also provided a technology for such training. At the same time, the emergence of newer technology, especially in the career area, provided a viable and important function for use of students who could act as teachers and facilitators who could enable others to make use of these developments. Structured programs, an innovation in the early 1970s, have become a solid and important component of services in most centers (Barr and Keating, 1979). Agencies, faced with having to choose among many well-developed and useful programs at a time of stable or declining professional resources, see in paraprofessionals a way to offer services in an efficient and cost-effective manner.

Paraprofessionals, it would seem, are here to stay as partners with professional staff in providing services to an increasingly diverse and service-oriented student population. This chapter will build on the statements of Ender in Chapter One to explore areas of importance for the design and implementation of paraprofessional programs in counseling and career agencies. This chapter discusses goals and functions; appropriate planning and implementation, especially of training and supervision; and systems issues. Information on viable, well-grounded programs concludes the chapter.

Goals and Functions

"The counseling center as a private preserve of certified professionals is becoming an anachronism" (Aiken and others, 1974, p. 480). Indeed, as early as 1970, the Task Force on Paraprofessionals (Invitational Conference of University and College Counseling Centers, 1970, p. 1) reminded its members that "implementation of a therapeutic community necessitates identification, training, and consultation with a number of persons who have not necessarily had prior professional training in counseling but who do perform therapeutic functions in the course of their daily experiences."

As early as 1966, Zunker and Brown demonstrated the effectiveness of student-to-student counselors in academic adjustment guidance. Research has demonstrated that paraprofessionals are effective in a wide range of other counseling areas: assertive training groups (Wasserman and others, 1975), working individually with students to develop appropriate social and study skills (Wasserman and others, 1975), and leading social anxiety management groups (Barrow and Hetherington, 1981). McKee and others (1977) reported that community college counselors accepted the use of guidance and product-oriented functions by paraprofessionals, but most believed that counseling and process-oriented functions should continue to be the responsibility of professional counselors. Crane and others, (1975) indicated that the use of paraprofessionals was acceptable to almost all counseling center directors, but there was disagreement regarding functions. In actual practice, most centers used paraprofessionals for help with only four student problem areas: freshman orientation, study skills, college adjustment, and drug problems. More recent data (Salovey, 1983) confirm all but the drug area, which has slipped as a top function and been replaced by services to minority students (48 percent) and women (39 percent) and by career (35 percent) and general psychological counseling (34 percent).

Data from this and other surveys do not spell functions out in detail. However, when this information is combined with reports from a number of active programs, it seems safe to say that paraprofessionals are firmly established as disseminators of information, especially in the academic and career areas. They also offer a number of structured groups and workshops in these areas. In personal and interpersonal areas, paraprofessionals are most frequently used to lead or colead groups based on behavior and social learning principles: assertion, anxiety reduction, weight control. In the academic, career, and personal concern areas, some individual advising and counseling (generally very short-term) is being done in the majority of programs studied.

Career services, whether housed in counseling centers or independently, are using large numbers of paraprofessionals. The fact that a number of career agencies were either established or reorganized in the past decade allowed them to introduce paraprofessionals from the start of their operation.

A primary goal for the use of paraprofessionals has been the extension of services to students, although the other goals that Ender articulates in Chapter One are also important. Another goal, less often explicitly stated, is to relieve professionals of tasks that they find boring or less fulfilling. Indeed, this can be a legitimate goal, in that paraprofessionals, performing a service for the first time, can bring enthusiasm and vigor that few professionals can bring after three or four years.

Paraprofessionals are proving especially valuable in identifying and serving the needs of so-called underserved populations or of groups with which no member of the professional staff has established an identification and services. In these cases, the paraprofessionals themselves are members of the population. Examples include women, veterans, older-than-average, gay, handicapped, and ethnic minority students.

For services to specific groups, membership in that group is essential. Many agencies also attempt to increase the diversity of agency personnel by employing paraprofessionals who have characteristics (for example, gender, age, ethnicity) that professional staff do not have. Higher education is now in a time of steady state, and opportunities to employ additional professional staff are few. Use of paraprofessionals allows agencies to provide additional help and to increase the representation in agency staff.

Planning and Implementation

Selection and Training. In general, counseling and career centers look for students who possess the characteristics articulated in Chapter One. They usually increase the emphasis on interpersonal sensitivity and skills, especially if paraprofessionals are to do any individual or small-group counseling work.

It is very helpful if the program can be built so that the final selection is not made until students have received some training, and their general style plus their ability to learn required skills can be evaluated. A highly recommended approach is to limit recruitment and selection to a training experience and then to make the final selection after the training. This works especially well if the training can be offered as an academic course. Students who are not selected can still earn credit and have a valuable learning experience. This approach requires a good deal of time and expertise on the part of the professional trainer, but it pays off in highly qualified paraprofessionals and in valuable learning experiences for other students.

It should definitely be considered when paraprofessionals are to engage in counseling and other more complex activities, as is often the case at counseling and career centers. An added benefit for established programs is that experienced paraprofessionals can assume co-teaching responsibility in the training program under supervision and thus gain new competencies while performing a valuable service.

Some form of preservice training is considered necessary for all paraprofessionals in counseling and career work, regardless of when and how selection occurs. Recommended preservice training has four components: basic helping skills; ethics and standards; agency mission, policies, and functions; and some general or specific training for the function to be performed. Training in how to use ongoing training and supervision, material on student services in the college or university and as a profession, and student development theory are optional but very useful components. They can be included in in-service training if preservice training time is limited.

Of the recommended components, basic helping skills and specific job training are the most extensive in terms of time and resources. Trainers of paraprofessionals generally use one of the basic interpersonal skills programs (Ivey, 1971; Kagan, 1975; Egan, 1975) for teaching these skills. Meade (1978) presents an excellent critique of these models, which should be helpful to a trainer who is uncertain about the strengths and limitations of the various approaches. In essence, Meade recommends tying choice of model to the goals to be achieved. Trainers need to take training on this component very seriously, and in most cases, paraprofessionals in counseling and career centers will need more work in this area than paraprofessionals in many other student services agencies do.

Training in specific job functions should also begin during preservice training. During this period, it is especially important for counseling and career paraprofessionals to see professionals at work and to see how the function that they will perform fits into the agency's work. Since many counseling interventions are based on theories in the area of learning, social, or developmental psychology, students should be at least introduced to the basic theory and concepts underlying the service that they will offer.

The role of trainer is key for counseling and career center professionals who are involved in paraprofessional programs, and it is often a new role, even to experienced helpers. Training procedures should always follow a systematic competence-building sequence. Delworth and Moore (1974) build on Carkhuff's (1969) work to articulate a four-step training model:

Step one: Translate the helping skill into specific behavioral goals. That is, answer the question, What specific behaviors comprise effective and ineffective practice of the helping skill in question? Step two: Develop training procedures that explain the desired helping goals in sequence, that model the skill as effectively practiced, and that give students continuous feedback on performance until minimally acceptable competence is attained. Step three: Provide supervised practice in which helping skills learned in step two can be used with a variety of clients or client groups until minimally acceptable competence is attained on the basic core dimensions of help and on the specific helping strategies demanded or used with various client problems. Step four: Provide learning situations in which the important theoretical and practical literature can be studied and integrated with actual helping experiences.

Supervision. Ongoing, regular supervision is essential. The ethics and standards of the profession require it, especially when paraprofessionals work with individual students. Group supervision can work well, but at least some individual supervision is recommended, especially when each paraprofessional performs a somewhat different function. Thomas and Good-Benson (1978) stress the importance of individual supervision of assessment, training, and planning. They present a checklist for supervisors and suggest that those who answer in the affirmative have a clear understanding of supervision and should feel good about their work:

1. Have you clarified your expectations and agreed to a supervisory plan with your supervisees?
2. Do you show respect for your supervisees by being prompt for appointments and by not canceling sessions except in emergency situations?
3. Do you schedule supervision sessions at a time that does not interfere either with your other work or with the responsibilities of your supervisees?
4. Do you provide an atmosphere of openness that is nevertheless

private and confidential in order to foster the sharing of problems?
5. Are you alert to special needs for training or special personal problems?
6. Are you willing to confront supervisees when appropriate?
7. Do you have genuine concern for the well-being and development of your supervisees? (pp. 70–71)

Delworth and Yarris (1978) recommend developing a plan for ongoing supervision prior to the start of training, so that procedures can be explained and initiated during preservice training. If the supervisors are not the trainers, they can be brought into the program and introduced both to the training method and to the trainees. In some cases, it may be useful to initiate regular supervision prior to the end of preservice training. Supervision should definitely be well coordinated with in-service training.

Systems Issues

While paraprofessional programs in counseling and career centers are very similar to those in other student services agencies, a few probable differences are worth noting.

Impact on Center Staff. Most counseling services and, to a lesser extent, career services are staffed by professionals with the doctoral degree. This degree and the associated high level of socialization into the profession can initially present a barrier to a paraprofessional program. Highly educated professionals may have difficulty believing that anyone can do important parts of their job. Often, the threat is felt more intensely by graduate students, who may be required to take a number of academic courses before they are admitted to practicum and allowed to provide services that undergraduate paraprofessionals are already providing.

Ethics and Standards. Ethics and standards can create another area of difficulty. More than perahps any other arena within student affairs, counseling centers must deal with an array of ethical and legal issues. For one thing, most centers follow the ethics set out in the American Psychological Association's Standards for Providers of Psychological Services as well as the ethical statements of the American Association for Counseling and Development, the American College Personnel Association, and the National Association of Student Personnel Administrators. Centers may follow the standards of the International Association of Counseling Services as well. All these documents enumerate a wide variety of approved and disapproved policies and procedures, ranging from case confidentiality issues to specific injunctions on materials that must be made available to the public. Since many agencies also perform testing or research functions, there are additional standards to be followed.

These issues must be worked through with care and sensitivity if a paraprofessional program is to be successful in these highly professionalized settings. Job functions, training, and supervision must be clearly spelled out.

There should be a clear rationale for and description of the tasks performed by paraprofessionals, and training and evaluation should be clearly linked to job function. It is valuable for the professional in charge of the program to compile the ethical and standards statements that are specifically applicable to paraprofessionals in that setting. Such a list can then be discussed and examples can be given in both preservice and in-service training. In most cases (for example, confidentiality), paraprofessionals must adhere exactly to the ethics and standards set for professionals. In addition, however, they are often faced with ethical dilemmas that differ from those usually faced by professional staff (for example, social interaction with students who are agency clients). It is therefore helpful to formulate a specific set of guidelines with and for the paraprofessionals.

Each program is encouraged to formulate its own set of paraprofessional ethics. A sample of such a statement follows:

1. Overall, respect for the client and the client's feelings and needs should be of prime importance.
2. Confidentiality of situations, interactions, and insights must always be respected. (If paraprofessionals do not understand which material or interactions are confidential, they should discuss this problem with their supervisor or the program director.)
3. Consultations with supervisors or professionals about problems should be conducted in a private manner and a private place.
4. Any and all confidential written material must be kept in a place where it is accessible only to those who have a legitimate right to see it.
5. Paraprofessionals should be aware of the hazards to them, to clients, and to the agency of personal involvement with clients or helpees outside the helping relationship.
6. Generally, paraprofessionals should not have personal involvement outside the helping relationship (for example, by dating) while the paraprofessional is engaged in helping interactions with the client.
7. If problems or questions concerning the extent of a paraprofessional's personal involvement with a client arise, they should be directed to the paraprofessional's supervisor or the program director.

It is essential for trainers to help paraprofessionals, professionals, and graduate students to understand and appreciate each group's contribution to the fulfillment of agency objectives. With sensitivity, clear communication, and a good dose of patience, this aim can be accomplished.

A Look at Today and Tomorrow

Paraprofessionals are here to stay in counseling and career work. As needs grow and as programs are strengthened, both the numbers and the functions of paraprofessionals may well increase. The area has come a long way in the past fifteen years, in terms both of the quality and of the quantity of programs and services provided. Those involved can congratulate themselves.

Professionals and paraprofessionals should also pause to reflect on deficiencies and future directions. At least two concerns are highly visible. First, there is a dearth of research on paraprofessional effectiveness. Little has appeared since some solid studies in the mid sixties to mid seventies. The field may well be taking too much for granted, and certainly it will be an easy mark for those who attack programs. Almost nothing has been done to study the effects of paraprofessional programs on the paraprofessionals themselves, although great development is often claimed.

Second, although there has been progress in training, the current situation is far from satisfactory. Ender and Winston's (1984) finding that 28.9 percent of the programs in their survey reported less than five hours of training is simply not acceptable. That 26.1 percent of the counseling and career centers in their survey reported more than fifty hours of training is encouraging, but the largest percentage (34.8 percent) still remains in the six- to fifteen-hour range. There are serious questions of competence and ethics to be addressed here. We can hope that those of us involved in paraprofessional programs will find a way to expand our energy, time, and commitment so that we can address the pressing issues of research and training. Our work, enthusiastically begun in the seventies, still has many frontiers in the mid eighties.

Programs

There are a number of well-grounded and exciting paraprofessional programs in counseling and career centers. This chapter highlights unique features of some programs that sample the range of approaches currently being used. More information can be acquired by writing to the resource person associated with each program. The names and addresses of these resource persons are listed in Appendix A of this volume.

University of Missouri–St. Louis (Counseling Service). The University of Missouri–St. Louis program is funded through student activities fees, and it is a student organization. The peer counselors are responsible for submitting a budget proposal, participating in budget hearings, and lobbying for funds each year. They have a close relationship with the counseling service. The centers are housed in one suite of offices, and supervision is provided by counseling service staff. Students must complete a course, "The Helping Relationship," prior to selection as a peer, and if they are chosen, they take a second course, "Applied Skills." Approximately six to ten peers are employed for about ten hours a week at $3.85 per hour. Peers offer a number of structured workshops (for example, resume writing, career exploration), assist students in using the career library and the System of Interactive Guidance and Information (SIGI), and see students for brief personal counseling (no more than three sessions) under close supervision.

Whitman College, Walla Walla, Washington (Career Center). At Whitman College, undergraduate student paraprofessionals developed and now manage seven of the ten major programs in the Career Center—recruitment, internship, extern and career consultant, summer job, workshop, career resource, and communications. These students select, train, and manage their own committee members. Consequently, forty-five students are currently involved in the center's activities, teaching five different workshops, contacting and hosting recruiters, developing internships, and producing written guides and booklets. Members of the paraprofessional staff have also been involved in professional conference and consulting presentations. Training and supervision are provided through weekly individual and group meetings.

The University of Utah, Salt Lake (University Counseling Center). The rich and well-developed training and service sequence at the University of Utah's Salt Lake campus is an outstanding feature of this program. A five-quarter-long experience for students, the first quarter is a formal training class taken for credit. The second quarter provides job-specific training, and the student begins to provide some services. The three remaining quarters are heavily service-oriented, and the students are paid. New students are phased into the program twice a year. Extensive training and evaluation materials have been developed by the coordinator and other professional staff. Paraprofessionals perform a wide variety of services in the personal growth, career, and learning center areas of the center. They colead workshops, conduct screening interviews with prospective participants in structured workshops, make presentations on campus, co-teach career and learning skills classes, tutor students, offer seminars interpreting the results of the Strong-Campbell Interest Inventory, and participate in research groups.

University of Missouri–Columbia Career Planning and Placement Center. The University of Missouri–Columbia Career Planning and Placement Center runs a large and comprehensive program. Position descriptions, training, and competencies are clearly articulated, and announcements typically draw more than 200 applicants for approximately twenty-five positions. Paraprofessionals offer career counseling and a variety of workshops. They also perform a wide variety of functions, such as programming computers and laying out advertising. Paraprofessionals work approximately ten hours per week and earn about $1,000 for the academic year.

References

Aiken, J., Brownell, A., and Iscoe, I. "The Training and Utilization of Paraprofessionals in a College Psychological Service Center." *Journal of College Student Personnel,* 1974, *15* (7), 480–486.

Barr, M. J., and Keating, L. A. "Editors' Notes." In M. J. Barr and L. A. Keating (Eds.), *Establishing Effective Programs*. New Directions for Student Services, no. 7. San Francisco: Jossey-Bass, 1979.

Barrow, J., and Hetherington, C. "Training Paraprofessionals to Lead Social Anxiety Management Groups." *Journal of College Student Personnel*, 1981, *22,* 269–273.

Carkhuff, R. R. *Helping and Human Relations*. New York: Holt, Rinehart and Winston, 1969.

Crane, J., Anderson, W., and Kirchner, K. "Counseling Center Directors' Attitudes Toward Paraprofessionals." *Journal of College Student Personnel,* 1975, *16* (2), 119–122.

Delworth, U., and Moore, M. "Helper Plus Trainer: A Two-Phase Program for the Counselor." *Personnel and Guidance Journal,* 1974, *52* (6), 428–433.

Delworth, U., and Yarris, E. "Concepts and Processes for the New Training Role." In U. Delworth (Ed.), *Training Competent Staff*. New Directions for Student Services, no. 2. San Francisco: Jossey-Bass, 1978.

Egan, G. *The Skilled Helper: A Model for Systematic Helping and Interpersonal Relating*. Monterey, Calif.: Brooks/Cole, 1975.

Ender, S. C., and Winston, R. B., Jr. "A National Survey of Student Paraprofessional Utilization in Student Affairs." Unpublished manuscript, Kansas State University, 1984.

Invitational Conference of University and College Counseling Centers. *Task Force Report on Paraprofessionals*. Lexington, Ky., 1970.

Ivey, A. E. *Microcounseling: Innovations in Interviewer Training*. Springfield, Ill.: Thomas, 1971.

Kagan, N. *Interpersonal Process Recall: A Method of Influencing Human Interaction*. East Lansing: Michigan State University Educational Publication Services, 1975.

McKee, J.E., Harris, C. M., Rhodes, P., and York, L. "Paraprofessionals in the Community College." *Journal of College Student Personnel,* 1977, *18* (3), 231–238.

Meade, C. J. "Interpersonal Skills: Who, What, When, Why." In U. Delworth (Ed.), *Training Competent Staff*. New Directions for Student Services, no. 2. San Francisco: Jossey-Bass, 1978.

Salovey, P. "A Survey of Campus Peer Counseling Activities." Paper presented at a meeting of the National College Health Association, St. Louis, Missouri, May 1983.

Thomas, L. E., and Good-Benson, P. "Supervision: A Key Element in Training." In U. Delworth (Ed.), *Training Competent Staff*. New Directions for Student Services, no. 2. San Francisco: Jossey-Bass, 1978.

Wasserman, C. W., McCarthy, B. W., and Feurie, E. H. "Student Paraprofessionals as Behavior Change Agents." *Professional Psychology,* 1975, *6* (2), 217–223.

Zunker, V.G., and Brown, W. F. "Comparative Effectiveness of Student and Professional Counselors." *Personal and Guidance Journal,* 1966, *44* (7), 738–743.

Ursula Delworth is professor of counselor education at the University of Iowa. She is coauthor of Student Paraprofessionals: A Working Model for Higher Education *and the author of a number of other publications in this area.*

Mary Johnson is a doctoral student in counseling psychology at the University of Iowa.

As this sourcebook shows, student paraprofessional programming has seen widespread and significant changes since the early 1970s. However, much work needs to be done if this programming effort is to continue to have a positive impact on institutions of higher education and divisions of student affairs.

Recommendations for the Future

Steven C. Ender

As I pointed out in Chapter One, an overwhelming majority of colleges and universities are using student paraprofessionals in almost all student affairs departments and agencies. The authors of the chapters in this sourcebook have emphasized several themes that can help to guide practice in paraprofessional programming. Across program settings, the authors agree, quality program implementation has five features: First, it develops and disseminates program goals and paraprofessional position descriptions that focus on student clients' developmental concerns. Second, recruitment is active. Third, it uses systematic selection processes. Fourth, it views extensive training as a selection criterion. Fifth, it recognizes the importance of continued supervision and program evaluation. The data presented in Chapter One provide recent figures on the percentage of student affairs programs that are attending to these basic and necessary program areas. Paraprofessional training and program evaluation appear to have some major shortcomings. Also, if paraprofessional programming is to continue to be a useful staffing technique in student affairs, serious attention is needed in the areas of research, professional preparation in the paraprofessional area, and standards to guide future practice.

Paraprofessional Training

The amount of time devoted to beginning paraprofessionals' pre-service training continues to leave much to be desired. Program coordinators

S. Ender, R. Winston (Eds.). *Using Students as Paraprofessional Staff.* New
Directions for Student Services, no. 27. San Francisco: Jossey-Bass, September 1984.

must ask themselves what tasks they expect student paraprofessionals to perform. Counseling and making referrals are two of the top five activities presently being performed by student paraprofessionals (Ender and Winston, 1984). If paraprofessionals are to perform these two critical tasks competently, training programs must focus on rudimentary counseling and interviewing skills, developmental assessment techniques, and referral strategies.

Learning, demonstrating, and retaining beginning counseling skills cannot be accomplished in a short time. To become competent in these skills takes time and practice. If training programs are not extended, program coordinators cannot expect paraprofessionals to be competent counselors and interviewers. Asking students to perform tasks for which they are not adequately trained will result in frustration, confusion, and eventual program demise.

Training programs must also address the critical area of problem assessment and program intervention and referral strategies. Competent paraprofessionals must be able to discriminate types of student problems. Are they developmental, counseling, or remedial in nature? With this assessment, paraprofessionals must be able to gauge the student's level of stress and the student's ability to actively assist in the problem area. To be successful in the helping interaction, the paraprofessional must be able to perform three important helper tasks: accurately assess the nature of a student's concern, decide on an appropriate program intervention, or make timely referrals if the situation calls for skills and expertise outside the paraprofessional's training and ability. Training programs that fail to address these three skill areas are programming for paraprofessional confusion and student client dissatisfaction. If acceptable skill levels are to be reached, training formats should be extended to at least forty hours spread over a period of ten to fifteen weeks. Ideally, this training takes place under the auspices of an academic class, and taking the class is a criterion for selection.

Program Evaluation

The program evaluation data presented in Chapter One indicate that almost one half of all paraprofessional programs fail to evaluate their impact on student clients. The absence of formal and frequent program evaluation suggests the lack of clear-cut and measurable program objectives. Telling others that paraprofessionals are effective must be supported by objective program evaluation data. If at all possible, these evaluation data should be tied to institutional variables important to administrators and institutional leadership. For example, how does the work of paraprofessionals affect students' performance in classes, students' satisfaction with the institution, career awareness, students' use of institutional resources, advisees' satisfaction, and so forth? These issues are important to institutional leaders. For paraprofessional programs to be accountable and viable, program coordinators must show how their programs affect the mission of the institution.

Research

The need continues for research studies that measure the effectiveness of paraprofessionals in many different student affairs settings. Advocates of paraprofessionals' effectiveness have to rely on outdated research findings to support their claims. Many cite the early work of Carkhuff (1968) as evidence that paraprofessionals can be effective change agents in the helping interaction. This may be true, but few paraprofessional training programs come close to the forty hours of training that Carkhuff advocates.

More recent support for paraprofessionals comes from Durlak (1979), who reviewed forty-two research studies comparing the impact of paraprofessionals and professionals across many types of treatment settings. Durlak reached three conclusions: Paraprofessionals achieved clinical outcomes equal to or significantly better than those obtained by professionals; professionals' clinical skills are not necessarily superior to paraprofessionals' skills; and there is little information on the factors accounting for paraprofessionals' effectiveness. Of particular interest to the readers of this sourcebook is Durlak's assertion (p. 88) that "the strongest support for paraprofessionals has come from programs directed at the modification of adults' and college students' specific target problem." Readers should also note that Nietzel and Fisher (1981) have questioned the validity of Durlak's study. Those interested in outcome research (and many of us need to be) are urged to review these two studies for further insight and clarification.

An interesting research study would consider length of training and paraprofessional effectiveness across many different types of program variables. These variables could include student client satisfaction, paraprofessionals' confidence as they engage in their role, and the impact of training on the personal growth of paraprofessionals, to name only a few.

The impact of service as a paraprofessional on a student's growth and development also needs further research. An overwhelming majority of paraprofessional coordinators endorse the concept that paraprofessionals are affected positively in human development areas as a direct result of their work (Ender and Winston, 1984). Again, most of these claims seem to be based on subjective analysis and feedback from paraprofessionals. Objective data must accompany these claims. Moreover, if there is a relation between service and growth, we must ask whether the effect of participation on students' maturity differs with the type of program or whether service as a helping person is the primary variable in the reported change.

One research question that seems to have merit involves the longitudinal study of students who pursue a paraprofessional position, get the job, then serve as a paraprofessional for one or two years. Students who applied for the position but did not get the job could serve as the control group. Several developmental assessment instruments (Hanson, 1982) now available would provide excellent pre and post measures for such a study. The results might begin to indicate how much personal growth a paraprofessional experiences as a result of his or her involvement in that role.

Graduate Preparation Programs

Student personnel preparation programs must consider the widespread use of paraprofessionals and assure that the program of study addresses this programming technique. A course that would help graduate students to design and implement paraprofessional programs would be useful in preparing future student affairs professionals. Moreover, it would be desirable to assist graduate students who want to acquire the skills necessary to be a competent paraprofessional trainer to acquire them.

Many of the skills needed—group dynamics, communication skills, design of developmental programs, development of program goals and objectives—are already taught. An educational experience is needed that ties these isolated concepts together and applies them to the task of training others—in this case, student paraprofessionals—for helping roles. Paraprofessional training programs would be strengthened if graduate students were taught how to conceptualize and write training curriculums and models that focused on training goals, behavioral objectives for trainees, and training processes that achieved these objectives.

Standards

The Council for the Advancement of Standards for Student Services/Development Programs (CAS) must address paraprofessional programming in a comprehensive manner. An acceptable minimum set of standards to guide paraprofessional utilization and programming is greatly needed. It appears that the time has come for such a statement. We can hope that this sourcebook will help to provide the impetus needed for further CAS action in this area.

References

Carkhuff, R. R. "Differential Functioning of Lay and Professional Helpers." *Journal of Counseling Psychology,* 1968, *15,* 117–126.

Durlak, J. A. "Comparative Effectiveness of Paraprofessionals and Professional Helpers." *Psychological Bulletin,* 1979, *86* (1), 80–92.

Ender, S. C., and Winston, R. B., Jr. "A National Survey of Student Paraprofessional Utilization in Student Affairs." Unpublished manuscript, Kansas State University, 1984.

Hanson, G. R. (Ed.). *Measuring Student Development.* New Directions for Student Services, no. 20. San Francisco: Jossey-Bass, 1982.

Nietzel, M. T., and Fisher, S. G. "Effectiveness of Professional and Paraprofessional Helpers: A Comment on Durlak." *Psychological Bulletin,* 1981, *89* (3), 555–565.

Steven C. Ender is assistant professor and counselor in the Center for Student Development at Kansas State University. Actively involved in paraprofessional programs throughout his professional career, he has coauthored a training manual for paraprofessionals, and he has also been actively involved in training professionals who desire to implement paraprofessional programs.

APPENDIX A

Sources of Further Information
About Model Programs

Chapter Two: Student Paraprofessionals in the Learning Centers

University of Georgia: Rebecca Galvin, Tutorial Program Coordinator, 116 Clark Howell Hall, Athens, GA 30602, (404) 542-7575.

University of Pittsburg: Anne Massey, Math Specialist, Learning Skills Center, 310 William Pitt Union, Pittsburg, PA 15260, (412) 624-5481.

Chapter Three: Student Paraprofessionals in Academic Advising

University of Montana: Kitty Corak, Coordinator of Academic Advising and Student Retention, Center for Student Development, Missoula, MT 59812, (406) 243-2835.

University of Wisconsin - Eau Claire: Wes Habley, Director of Academic and Career Advising, 120 Schofield Hall, Eau Claire, WI 54701, (715) 836-3487.

Marymount Manhattan College: Sr. Margaret Ann Landry, Director, Academic Advising and Retention, 221 E 71st Street, New York, NY 10021, (212) 472-3800.

University of Wisconsin, Whitewater: John Prentice, Executive Director, Student Administrative Services, Whitewater, WI 53190, (414) 472-1570.

Chapter Four: Student Paraprofessionals in Residence Halls

Indiana University at Bloomington: John H. Schuh, Residential Life, Indiana University, 801 W Jordan, Bloomington, IN 47405, (812) 335-1764.

University of Wisconsin - Stevens Point: Susan Mitchell, Counseling Center, University of Wisconsin - Stevens Point, Stevens Point, WI 54481, (715) 346-4343.

Chapter Five: Orientation and the Role of the Student Paraprofessionals

Bentley College: Diane Austin, Counseling and Student Development, Beaver and Forest Street, Waltham, MA 02154, (612) 891-2272.

Bradley University: David H. Goldenberg, Division of Student Affairs, Peoria, IL 61625, (309) 676-7611.

Chapter Six: Student Paraprofessionals in Counseling/Career Centers

University of Missouri - St. Louis: Robert J. Carr, Director, Counseling Service, 8001 Natural Bridge Road, St. Louis, MO   63121, (314) 553-5711.

Whitman College: Iona M. Joiner, Director, Career Center, Walla Walla, WA   99362, (509) 527-5183.

The Univeristy of Utah: Edie Kochenour, Coordinator, Learning Center and Paraprofessional Program, University Counseling Center, 2120 Annex Building, Salt Lake City, UT   84112, (801) 581-6826.

University of Missouri - Columbia: Robert N. Hanson, Career Planning and Placement Center, Counseling Services, Columbia, MO   65211, (314) 882-6801.

APPENDIX B

Proposed Standards on Use of
Student Paraprofessionals in Student Affairs

Prepared by Steven C. Ender, Clifford G. Schuette, Carmen G. Neuberger

I. Purpose and Goals: Standards

   A. Paraprofessional student helpers are employed in many student affairs
   programs. These helpers are assigned to residence halls, counseling
   centers, learning/tutorial centers, academic advising programs, admissions offices, orientation programs, etc. For purposes of this statement, paraprofessionals are viewed as undergraduate students employed
   by a Division of Student Affairs for purposes of providing direct
   services to other students.

   The goals for utilization of paraprofessionals include:

   1. To provide direct services to college students.

   2. To maximize the potential positive effects of peers interacting and
      helping peers.

   3. To provide guidance and developmental support programs rather than
      counseling/therapeutic interventions. These programs and individ-
      ual services are designed to provide educational and preventive
      interventions rather than remedial.

   4. To provide a wide range of developmental services at a reduced cost
      to student affairs' staffing budgets.

   5. To provide student role models for other students to emulate in
      regard to self-responsible, self-directed behavior.

I. *Purpose and Goals: Interpretations*

   A. *Divisions of Student Affairs employ students to serve in many different
   capacities. Examples of student positions include: work study typ-
   ists, student aides working as file clerks and receptionists, student
   laborers painting residence halls or working with groundskeeping crews
   and paraprofessionals delivering educational services. This statement
   pertains to paraprofessionals only and is directed to student positions
   which are designed to deliver educational services to assist other
   students in adjusting, persuing, and experiencing satisfaction in the
   educational setting. Below is a brief interpretation of the five goals
   included in this statement.*

   1. *Paraprofessionals are working directly with other students either
      in a one-to-one or group format. They would also be found co-
      leading groups with other paraprofessionals and professionals.*

   2. *Institutions employing paraprofessionals realize the powerful
      developmental impact students have on one another and are inten-
      tionally structuring this impact in positive ways by initiating
      paraprofessional programs. Their contact with other students is
      planned and systematic. The relationship(s) between paraprofes-
      sionals and student clients is purposeful and goal/program orient-
      ed.*

   3. *The services provided are designed to assist in the developmental
      task completion of students in the target population. The func-
      tions while performing duties could be described with such words as
      assisting, teaching, and supporting rather than maintaining,
      re-training, or interpreting. Any contact with a student who is
      experiencing intrapersonal and remedial difficulties of a psycho-
      logical nature is out of the range of the paraprofessional's
      expertise.*

   4. *There are many services provided by full-time professional staff
      members which could be offered through paraprofessionals. Examples
      include: tutorial/study skills assistance, residence hall adjust-*

ment, utilization of career libraries, orientation to campus,
academic advising, etc. Colleges and universities which are
utilizing paraprofessionals are attempting to provide services in
many areas which focus on developmental task resolution. Providing
developmental interventions for large and significant percentages
if the student body through professional staff members are usually
impossible and therefore student paraprofessionals are employed to
attempt wider impact on the total student population without
experiencing a great increase in staffing budgets.

5. Students employed by the student affairs departments should be able
to model the outcome behaviors the department is attempting to
facilitate in other students. For example, study skills paraprofessionals would have adequate study skills and resident assistants
would demonstrate behaviors which are conducive to living successfully in residence halls.

II. Human Resources: Standards

A. The paraprofessional is an individual without extensive training in the
helping professions but who is specifically selected, trained, and
given on-going supervision in the performance of some designated
portion of the task(s) usually performed by a professional. While this
person can relieve the professional to perform tasks of a more complex
nature, it is important to realize the function is an educational
rather than remedial one. It is the educational focus of the position
which should guide the use of this invaluable human resource.

B. The professional has a responsibility to insure that the role is
carefully defined so that expectations do not exceed capabilities.
Correspondingly, the job description must avoid focusing on menial
tasks which are not reflective of the educational training experi-
ence(s).

C. Students serving must model utilization of preventive developmental
growth strategies. These helpers are individuals who are actively
exploring themselves as human beings, assessing their present levels of
developmental growth and taking advantage of institutional programs,
services, and resources.

D. As staff members, they should be representative of the population they
serve. This holds true for sex, race, age, and demographical factors.
Sharing the environment of those they work with contributes to effectiveness and aids communication. Students receiving help and assistance from paraprofessional student helpers need to have choices as to
who will assist them. This is made possible through a heterogenous
peer helper staff. The ratio of peer helper to student receiving
services should not exceed 1 to 35.

E. Qualifications: Paraprofessionals must be selected with attention
given to the following areas: academic record; recommendations from
faculty, staff, and other student helpers; past and present leadership
experiences; and a desire and willingness to assist and help other
students. Students serving should receive systematic training in
helping skills and personal growth strategies. It is strongly recommended that training be given prior to selection.

F. Training: Training, at the minimum, must cover the following areas if
the paraprofessional is to be in a position to implement student
development strategies for themselves and others. Extensive initial
training and on-going in-service training is recommended. Areas of
training include: knowledge of the paraprofessional role; awareness of
self and the power of modeling behavior for those students with whom
they have contact; community support skills, student (human) development theory; communication skills and the helping interaction; goals
setting/behavioral objectives; assessment skills and techniques;
cross-cultural relations; study skills' techniques; knowledge of campus
and community resources and referral techniques. Other areas of
training should be added as determined by the specific services provided to the student consumer and the area of their work assignment.

II. Human Resources: Interpretations

A. Implementation of paraprofessional staffs takes considerable thought
and preparation. The department sponsoring this programming thrust
must pay particular attention to such human resources issues as recruitment, training, selection, and evaluation.

B. The role should focus on the central programming theme of the department employing the paraprofessional. That is, those working in the
career counseling office should be assisting other students with career
related concerns as the primary focus of their job responsibilities.
This is not to say that they should not be typing, duplicating materials, or compiling evaluation data from time to time. All of these
functions are necessary for program implementation and follow-up.
However, clerical functions should not be the major focus of the
position.

C. Students in the paraprofessional role should demonstrate their concern
for their personal growth and development. That is, they should be
encouraged to take advantage of campus resources and other activities
which will contribute to their success as students and productive
citizens. Supervisors can contribute to this process by offering
in-service training experiences which respond to their needs as helpers
and students. Paraprofessionals should be encouraged to model adap-
tive, responsible behaviors which will contribute to their success as
college students.

D. Program administrators should strive to recruit and select students who
represent various backgrounds to serve on the paraprofessional staff.
If possible students receiving services should feel some personal
identification with the individual providing the service. Students
receiving services should also feel comfortable switching to a different helper than the one initially offering the service if this would
result in better utilization of the information offered by the sponsoring department.

A ratio of peer helpers to students receiving services of 1 to 35 on a
weekly basis is proposed. This number may be somewhat higher if the
paraprofessional is performing orientation functions (especially if
they are conducting tours) but would be lower if the bulk of the work
was one to one (e.g., study skills counseling or tutorial work). If
this is the situation the weekly ratio would be 1 to 12 and should
never exceed 1 to 15. This is a maximum of individual clients as the
paraprofessional work should be limited to 12 to 15 hours weekly.

E. The ideal student to be selected to become a paraprofessional is one
who has mastered the outcome objectives of the service area. For
example, the ideal tutor in the institution's developmental academic
program would be a past program participant who has successfully
completed the program and has been mainstreamed into the regular
academic curriculum. The more the paraprofessional can personally
identify with the needs and concerns of the target population the more
effective he or she will be. As it is sometimes impossible to select
among representatives of the target population other students can and
should be given consideration for the position(s).

The students academic record will have a bearing on selection, be
somewhat dependent on the position, and must be attended to as he/she
delivers program services. Higher academic records would be expected
of peer tutors and study skill counselors (3.0 or above). Others
should strive to maintain an overall average of 2.5 on a four point
scale and should not be allowed to continue on the staff if the
average slips below 2.0.

Letters of recommendations from faculty, staff, and other paraprofessionals are very important. This endorsement of potential staff
members helps to create institutional commitment for the program and
assists in creating a recruitment network for the peer program.
Administrators must strive to follow up on recommendation resources
thanking these individuals for supporting the potential paraprofessional and ultimately the program.

In most cases potential paraprofessionals should be able to demonstrate
past leadership experiences in the high school or college setting.
These experiences could result in participation in activities such as
clubs and organizations, church, the scouts, athletics, hospital
volunteers, etc. On the other hand, some students may not have
extensive past experiences in leadership or helping roles. These
students should not be overlooked, but screened carefully to ascertain
their potential to be a helper to others.

F. Areas of training, as outlined in the standards statement comprise
generic helping skills and processes applicable to all peer helper
training programs. These areas would be best presented in an academic
course for credit and could be offered by schools and colleges in
education or the liberal arts. Potential departments offering these
courses would include counselor education, psychology, home economics,
sociology, and social work. It is suggested that individuals responsible for training develop relationships with faculty representing one
or more of these academic areas requesting their assistance in developing the training curriculum and co-teaching the training course.

Training through a course format is the ideal method but may be impossible on many college campuses. These standards would recommend some
sort of reimbursement for participation in training. If credit is
impossible, other methods similar to the reimbursement offered in the
work setting is recommended (money, room and board, tuition waiver,
etc.). Training should last a minimum of 40 hours of student/trainer
contact and be offered utilizing many training methodologies (didactic
lecture, experiential learning, role plays, utilization of video and
audio tape feedback exercises, etc.). All programs should also offer
continuing in-service training programs.

III. Programs/Services/Activities: Standards

A. The content of these areas must be determined by the specific student
affairs program employing the paraprofessional. It is important to
stress that the program, service, or activity performed should be
developmental and preventive in nature rather than remedial.

B. Examples of Programs/Services/Activities involving paraprofessionals
are: Orientation, Academic Advising, Academic Skills Tutoring, Admissions, Registrar and Financial Aid Programs, International Student
Services and Community Involvement Activities such as Big Buddy,
Hotline and Companion Programs.

III. Programs/Services/Activities: Interpretations

A. As stated, paraprofessionals are employed to work in student affairs
departments to deliver programs and services which will enhance other
students' higher educational experience. These services are developed
and implemented to assist students in educational satisfaction, adjustment, and persistence.

B. Examples of services provided by paraprofessionals include orientation,
tours of campus, assisting students with academic registration, providing academic tutoring and study skills assistance, providing emotional
support through crises lines, helping students adjust to residence hall
living, etc.

IV. Facilities: Standards

A. The very nature of paraprofessional activities demands that flexibility
exists when it comes to the provision of appropriate physical facilities. They do not typically need private offices but such facilities
should be available as the need arises. In general, three different
aspects demand consideration with regard to facilities. These can be
best put in terms of three questions.

B. What is the paraprofessional expected to do? Like any human service
delivery system, the facilities must be conducive to the particular
endeavor.

C. What are the circumstances which will protect and enhance the well-being of the clientele served by the paraprofessional? Care must be taken to protect the rights and privileges of the clientele.

D. What are the circumstances which will protect and enhance the well-being of the paraprofessional? Care must be taken to protect the paraprofessional from personal risk or injury.

IV. *Facilities: Interpretations*

A. *Since paraprofessionals are used in many different activities and service areas it is not possible to specify one standard setting to which all programs are to adhere. The overall principal when evaluating paraprofessional programs is one of appropriateness. The task of the paraprofessional should be central to the sponsoring agency's task and the paraprofessional's status should avoid a "second class" position. Facilities then should be judged on the basis of the following criteria.*

B. *Facilties should be appropriate for the task to be performed. To do any job, professional or paraprofessional, an individual must have the physical setting conducive to performing the task well. Evaluations should consider the adequateness of areas for relaxation as well as for work. In addition, the impact of the paraprofessional's task on the setting of other students, faculty, professionals, or paraprofessionals. In other words, the paraprofessional's activities should not distructively infringe upon other individual's space.*

C. *In the case where the paraprofessional is directly involved with the delivery of services to individuals or groups, several concerns exist. If the service demands client confidentiality, the facitlies must provide the privacy necessary for such confidentiality. If confidentiality is not always necessary, it is simply necessary for facilities to be available when the need arises.*

D. *It is necessary to provide the paraprofessional with facilities which allows him/her to do his/her job. The working environment should convey to the paraprofessional that the work he/she does is important to the sponsoring agency. Facilities should not place the paraprofessional in physical, psychological, or ethical jeopardy.*

V. Financial and Other Resources: Standards

A. Student paraprofessionals must be rewarded for their services as would any one working in a service area. There are many reward alternatives. Direct monetary payment; tuition remission; fee waiver; room and board; and academic credit for the services performed are examples of reward options.

V. *Financial and Other Resources: Interpretations*

A. *The type of reimbursement will be dependent upon such factors as institutional policy, nature of the position, number of hours worked per week, etc. Regardless of these factors they should be reimbursed fairly for their services. If money is the reward system utilized, minimum wage is sufficient with possible increases for second and third year staff members. If the paraprofessional is working under a volunteer status these services should be recognized at award ceremonies, documentation in permanent files, and recommendation to future employers.*

VI. Relationships with Faculty and Other Groups and Agencies: Standards

A. The supervising professional has a responsibility to carefully delineate the organizational relationship to which the paraprofessional belongs. This is important. If the paraprofessional does not understand his/her relationship to the institution at large, misunderstandings will likely arise.

B. Lines of work responsibilities and specific duties should be articulated so that both paraprofessionals and professionals have a clear concept as to the services provided by each. Each paraprofessional should have one professional supervisor with whom they maintain a close working relationship. Formal contact between these two individuals should be initiated on a weekly basis, and more often as necessary. The paraprofessional should never be allowed to deliver services without on-going professional supervision.

C. Paraprofessionals should model for other students the ability to communicate and associate with both faculty and staff at the institution.

VI. *Relationships with Faculty and Other Groups and Agencies: Interpretations*

A. *It is necessary for the paraprofessional to fully understand his/her role in the employing organization. Care needs to be taken to carefully specify the job description and it should also be in writing. The paraprofessional should also have an understanding of how his/her job description varies from other paraprofessionals as well as professionals, faculty, and/or agencies.*

B. *Central to the concept of paraprofessionalism is the notion of supervision by a professional. The term "professional" can include a range of individuals. Persons who are graduate assistants, graduate teaching assistants and interns may comprise one end of the professional continuum. They should have had some previous experience and currently be engaged in some appropriate area of graduate education. The other end of the professional continuum would include individuals with pertinent experience and who hold the masters' or doctorate in one of the human service disciplines. A formal supervision program needs to be operational. Supervision of paraprofessionals can be in groups or individually depending on the duties of the position.*

C. *The quality of the paraprofessional necessarily includes being a good example to others by relating in ways that exhibit interpersonal awareness, assertiveness, and empathy. The paraprofessional is in fact expected to display an ability to relate to the various agency publics with a high degree of competency.*

VII. Planning: Standards

A. Planning for the use of paraprofessionals should begin early in the academic year for the following year in order to provide for budgetary, staff, and facilities requirements. Long-range planning should be based on evaluative studies of the entire paraprofessional program.

VII. *Planning: Interpretations*

A. *This documentation would include the program's goals and objectives, recruitment and selection procedures, training requirements and the method(s) of compensation and evaluation. The content of these areas should parallel those points addressed in these standards, modified to meet individual institution and program needs. Program administrators should pay special attention to the aspect of time management in the planning process. If paraprofessionals are to be recruited, selected, and trained prior to employment, a start up time of six to eight months is essential when implementing new paraprofessional programs and when one is selecting new staff for an existing program.*

VIII. Evaluation: Standards

A. A clear statement of evaluation criteria should be written and distributed to all paraprofessional staff members. They should know how, when, and by what criteria they will be evaluated. Evaluation should be viewed and communicated as a developmental learning opportunity and not as a threat to one's self-esteem. Evaluation should take place at least twice during each academic year. The second of these evaluations

should determine whether or not a paraprofessional should be continued
on the staff for the following academic year.

VIII. *Evaluation: Interpretations*

A. *Informal evaluation sessions (formative) between supervisors and
paraprofessionals should take place on a continuous basis. The feedback which would occur during these supervisory sessions would be the
result of supervisor observation, client feedback and paraprofessional
concerns for individuals in the target population. These sessions
could take the tone of mentoring between the supervisor and paraprofessional focusing not only on the program participants but also the
growth and development of the paraprofessional.*

*The two formal evaluation sessions would be specifically designed to
evaluate the effectiveness of the paraprofessional. These evaluation
sessions should focus on the objectives outlined in the behavioral job
description as criterion for feedback. The first of these sessions
would outline the strengths and weaknesses in relationship to job
performance. Specific areas which need improvement should be articulated to the paraprofessional. Methods and strategies to reach these
performance levels should be highlighted and discussed. If at all
possible, a contract between the supervisor and paraprofessional should
be formulated outlining the behavior to be changed, strategies for
changing it, and the date the change will be completed.*

*The second formal evaluation session should take place near the end of
the academic year for the purposes of re-hiring for the next academic
year. Success or failure in regards to the contracting which took
place in the first evaluation session would have direct bearing on the
outcome of session two.*

IX. Ethics: Standards

A. Ethical considerations must be identified, disseminated to, and discussed with all student paraprofessionals. Ethically, they should
report to their supervisor any concern arising from contact with a
student with which the paraprofessional feels unqualified to handle.
They should not be put in the position of interpreting psychological
tests to students. They should never be employed to offer services in
the place of a professional staff member whose qualifications and
training are necessary to perform the service, program, or activity.

B. The paraprofessional must recognize the limitations of his/her knowledge and skills, seek improvement via additional training and supervision, and refer the student to the professional when skills or experience are inadequate. Given this framework, the paraprofessional is
expected to act in accordance with the following guidelines:

1. While not a professional, the paraprofessional accepts that he/she
   is expected to uphold standards of behavior consistent with the
   profession which he/she is serving.

2. The primary concern of the paraprofessional is the dignity and
   welfare of the individual.

3. The paraprofessional must become familiar with both campus and
   community resources available to those being served.

4. The paraprofessional must make explicit, to students whom they come
   in contact with, the services he/she is able to provide and should
   avoid acting beyond the realm for which he/she was selected and
   trained.

5. The paraprofessional needs to recognize his/her limitations and
   make appropriate referrals when necessary.

6. The paraprofessional is expected to adhere to the confidentiality
   policy of the sponsoring agency. They should always operate within
   the framework of general institutional policies and procedures.

IX. *Ethics: Interpretations*

A. *Evaluating ethical concerns in the paraprofessional role takes a subjective eye. The overall concern is that the paraprofessional know the limits of his/her training, duties, and abilities. By definition, paraprofessionals perform some of the tasks that are in the domain of the professional but with appropriate training and supervision. One exception is in the area of psychological testing. Due to the intricate nature of such testing and the critical need for accurate interpretation, paraprofessionals should not engage in such activity. Training paraprofessionals in psychological testing simply is not feasible in terms of time and complexity and it would probably violate professional (APGA & APA) codes of ethics.*

B. *Ethical guidelines should be covered in the paraprofessional training program. Guidelines have been provided in the standards section and should be used as a sample, not as a definite ethical code which all paraprofessionals must use. Evaluating paraprofessional's understanding of ethical conduct could probably be best accomplished with individual interviews and by reviewing paraprofessional training materials.*

X. Legal Issues: Standards

A. Institutions may be held legally responsible for services performed by paraprofessionals. Issues of liability, confidentiality and non-discrimination must be carefully covered in training.

X. *Legal Issues: Interpretations*

A. *Program administrators must be aware of the legal implications involved when implementing student paraprofessional staffed programs. As professional staff, they are accountable for the actions of the students they supervise.*

Index